D1570713

D. SANTIAGO VIDAURRI,

Gobernador de Nuevo-Leon.

Ronnie C. Tyler

SANTIAGO VIDAURRI

AND THE SOUTHERN CONFEDERACY

TEXAS STATE HISTORICAL ASSOCIATION

Copyright © 1973 by Ronnie C. Tyler

L.C. Card Number: 73–186709

ISBN 0–87611–029–4

FOR MOM AND DAD

CONTENTS

ILLUSTRATIONS

ACKNOWLEDGEMENTS

Santiago Vidaurri's name turns up in almost every study of the Texas-Mexico border during the decades of the 1850's and 1860's. But usually he is only mentioned, with little information given about him or the role he played in governing northern Mexico during almost ten years. He is inevitably called "general," "Lord of the North," or a "powerful governor." Even if his military and political exploits are briefly recounted, no reference is given to the unique situation that allowed him to become so powerful. For several years Vidaurri exercised virtually independent control of Nuevo León y Coahuila, fielding his own army, negotiating with President Benito Juárez, and conducting what amounted to foreign relations. In his strong adherence to regionalism Vidaurri continued a long tradition of independence in Nuevo León.

Any study of this sort cannot be undertaken without the aid of many helpful people and organizations. A grant from the Texas Good Neighbor Commission enabled me to study at the Instituto Tecnológico y de Estudios Superiores de Monterrey. Professor Edward H. Moseley of the University of Alabama generously shared his research on Santiago Vidaurri. Lic. Israel Cavazos Garza of the Archivo General de Estado de Nuevo León and Ing. Isidro Vizcaya Canales of the Instituto Tecnológico y de Estudios Superiores de Monterrey offered guidance and counseled with me on various aspects of the history of Nuevo León. Lic. Santiago Roel, Jr., allowed me to use the Vidaurri papers in his private collection, which were invaluable in understanding certain events. The reference staffs of the Texas Christian University and Austin College libraries and Mrs. Nancy Wynne and Mrs. Margaret McLean of the Amon Carter Museum of

11

Western Art Library were most helpful in assembling research materials.

Professors Donald E. Worcester and Malcolm D. McLean of Texas Christian University and Lawrence R. Murphy of the American University in Cairo read the manuscript and offered numerous useful suggestions. Dean Dan T. Bedsole of Austin College provided funds from the Faculty Research Fund for the pictorial resources. Diane Bertram compiled the index and Steve Schuster prepared the map. Finally, I would like to thank Mary Shields Pearson for her many helpful comments.

RONNIE C. TYLER
Fort Worth, August, 1973

Chapter I

THE ARCHITECT OF REGIONALISM

As they met in Monterrey on February 14, 1864, the governor of Nuevo León y Coahuila and the Mexican President represented two completely opposing governmental philosophies. President Benito Juárez, leading a motley band of patriots in an effort to escape from the French interventionists, inspired great idealism as he attempted to weld widely diverse forces into a nation. He hoped for a strong, centralized government and for reforms in the poverty-stricken, church-dominated Mexican society that was so near defeat at the hands of native conservatives and invading Frenchmen. Governor Santiago Vidaurri, on the other hand, was the leading *caudillo* in the northern states. He had argued for states' rights and for a federalist system of government for almost nine years.

Their interview did not take the form of a political debate. Rather, it was an exchange between two desperate men. The President had moved from city to city, staying just ahead of the oncoming French army. He needed Monterrey, the leading city of the north, as his headquarters. He also needed the customs revenue of the state of Nuevo León y Coahuila to finance his administration. Vidaurri was engaged in a struggle just as frenetic. He had fought for years to maintain his regional independence, but now he was threatened from two sides. He could submit to Juárez or he could submit to the French, who were closing in from the east.

If Vidaurri hoped to preserve his informal title of "Lord of the North," as he had repeatedly in years past, he would be forced to ally with the French. At least there was hope that they would allow him to remain as governor. But Juárez would severely limit his independent manner of governing and presumably demand his resignation. Now, as he talked with the President, Vidaurri

therefore defended his autonomy, indicating that he would allow
Juárez neither to collect the customs duties nor to establish his
headquarters in Monterrey and keep his army there. Obviously
there would be no agreement. The interview had lasted only a
few minutes when Governor Vidaurri's son, Indalecio, excitedly
drew his pistol, shouting that his father should rebel and end the
flight of the hapless President. Juárez had expected a confrontation, but undoubtedly he was shaken as he and his party hastily
retreated to their carriages and returned to Saltillo. Vidaurri later
joined the French in their effort to win the Empire of Mexico
for Maximilian, the Hapsburg archduke from Austria.[1]

The rather unusual encounter of the two leaders came about
because of a unique situation that had developed on the Texas-
Mexico border. Northern Mexico historically had been closer to
Texas than Mexico City because lack of communication, roads
that regularly succumbed to bad weather, and unfavorable ter-
rain between Monterrey and the interior had led the agrarian and
mining interests in the north to look for easier routes to market.
As the Spanish boundary receded, first from Louisiana, then to
the Rio Grande following the Mexican War, Monterrey found itself nearer the frontier and more able to participate in the illicit
trade that developed with the resourceful traders and merchants
who had settled in Texas following independence and statehood.[2]

Northern Mexico was, relatively speaking, a poor area that
needed regularized commerce and industry to realize its full
potential. Agricultural endeavors were continually plagued by
disease or drought. The mines that had stimulated so much settlement and interest during the colonial period were either exhausted or too poor to make extraction profitable. Many wealthy
families, therefore, had turned to ranching or trade to make their

---

[1] José María Iglesias, *Revistas históricas sobre la intervención francesa en
México*, 268–270; Guillermo Prieto, *Lecciones de historia patria escritas para
los alumnos del colegio militar*, 503; Carlos Pérez-Maldonado (ed.), "La
pugna Juárez-Vidaurri en Monterrey—1864," *Memorias de la Academia Mexicana de la Historia*, XXIV (enero-marzo, 1965), 73–74.

[2] Joseph Milton Nance, *After San Jacinto: The Texas-Mexican Frontier,
1836–1841*, 78–82, 100–112, 470–476, and *Attack and Counterattack: The
Texas-Mexican Frontier, 1842*, 4, 18, 79, 117, 119, 206.

fortunes.[3] When the Union navy blockaded the Southern ports during the Civil War in the United States, leaving northern Mexico as the only outlet (besides blockade running, which was much more dangerous) through which the Confederacy could trade with Europe and the rest of the world, the Mexican states along the Texas border were prepared to take advantage of an unprecedented commercial boom. During this period many merchants and politicos established bases for fortunes that still endure.

By mid-1861 another factor contributed greatly to the prosperity of northern Mexico: Governor Vidaurri had constructed a political environment that allowed him control of and profit from the trade. He had power over the bureaucracies of Nuevo León, Coahuila, and Tamaulipas, the three states through which trade goods had to pass to gain access to the Gulf of Mexico.

The man who was able to defy his president, the man who governed northern Mexico for nine years, was an enigma to many. An aura of mystery surrounds his birthplace, parents, and early life. Vidaurri himself might have been expected to clear up some of the questions during his lengthy public career, but on the rare occasions when he reminisced, he spoke only for public consumption, couching his words in the most patriotic—and sometimes vague—language. The date and place of his birth, education, and much of his later career are largely unknown or the subject of controversy.

Romantic legends persist in northern Coahuila that he was an Indian, and perhaps twelve or fourteen years old when he was captured and cared for by a sympathetic Mexican family in Santa Rosa, Coahuila.[4] His first years were spent in the nearby village of Múzquiz, however, encouraging speculation that this was his birthplace.[5] Later he lived much of his youth near Monclova, onetime capital of Coahuila, leading some to believe that he was born there.[6] Yet documents seem to prove otherwise. According

[3] Santiago Roel, *Nuevo León: apuntes históricos*, 115–116.
[4] Oscar Flores Tapia, *Coahuila: la reforma, la intervención y el imperio*, 25–26.
[5] Roel, *Nuevo León*, 134 n.
[6] *El Restaurador de la Libertad* (Monterrey), August 11, 1855.

15

to Santiago Roel, his first biographer, he was born in the Nuevo León village of Lampazos on July 25, 1808.[7] While the place is correct, the date apparently is erroneous, since the document upon which the reference is based clearly indicates 1809 as the year of birth.[8] The confusion surrounding Vidaurri's early years likely was to his benefit. Northerners could thus imagine that Vidaurri had been born wherever they wanted. Perhaps Vidaurri even encouraged the various rumors in order to take advantage of the extreme loyalty to region in Mexico.

A few facts about Vidaurri, however, are well documented. He rose to prominence in a conservative government and first gained public attention in 1832 by cutting off a soldier's hand, an action which does not portend political greatness. But he was placed in jail where he quickly attracted the attention of the jailor because of his literacy. After serving for a time as scribe of the municipal jail, Vidaurri was promoted to chief clerk, a position he held until 1837. In that year he was made *oficial mayor* (chief assistant) to Governor Joaquín García, a conservative who had received his appointment from a conservative president, Anastasio Bustamante. García held little real power at that time because the Constitution of 1836 had stripped the states of most of their powers.[9]

The next several years were a time of struggle between the conservatives (centralists) and the liberals (federalists). President Bustamante was ousted in 1841 by a junta of generals who felt he was not sufficiently in control of the country. Manuel María de Llano, former congressman and enthusiastic liberal, was named governor of Nuevo León by the ruling military chieftains in Monterrey, Colonel José María Ortega and General Mariano Arista. Vidaurri became the new governor's secretary.[10]

[7] Santiago Roel (ed.), *Correspondencia particular de D. Santiago Vidaurri, gobernador de Nuevo León* (1855–1864), vii.

[8] See the baptismal record in Volume III, citation number 282, of Lampazos, N. L., Archivo Parroquial, Bautismos, Vols. I–III: 1700–1829. Apparently this is the same document cited in Roel, *Correspondencia*, vii, note 1; and in Leopoldo Naranjo (ed.), *Lampazos, sus hombres, su tiempo, sus obras*, 115.

[9] Roel, *Correspondencia*, vii–viii; Roel, *Nuevo León*, 133–134, 137–138, 157.

[10] Roel, *Nuevo León*, 127, 137–138; Antonio Morales Gómez, *Cronología de Nuevo León, 1527–1955*, 167, 171.

Vidaurri probably first became acquainted with Texas when he was sent there in 1841 to spy on the Texan Santa Fé expedition for General Arista, commander of the Army of the North. The expedition was a "politico-military-commercial" venture sponsored by Texas President Mirabeau B. Lamar in an effort to divert a portion of the lucrative Santa Fé Trail trade to Texas and to establish Texan control of the New Mexico area. New Mexico Governor Manuel Armijo was alerted that the Texans were coming, and he arrested them upon their arrival at Laguna Colorado, near present-day Tucumcari.[11]

Vidaurri had proved himself a competent scout. He returned to Mexico and served under a conservative governor during the hectic years from 1843 to 1845 and again from 1853 to 1855. By 1855 he exercised considerable influence among a group of newcomers to the state's politics–Ignacio Zaragoza, José Silvestre Aramberri, Mariano Escobedo, Lázaro Garza Ayala, Francisco Naranjo, and Juan Zuazua and others–who had grown tired of the inept government that had plagued the state since Mexico's defeat at the hands of the United States in 1848. They were trying to rid Mexico of the disastrous forces that had taken advantage of the poverty-stricken populace through a corrupt church and a despotic government and consequently rendered the country incapable of meeting the American challenge. Vidaurri and his followers, in short, were the core of a developing liberal movement in the north.[12]

Being also an opportunist, Vidaurri saw his chance to seize power in the spring of 1855 when Mexico erupted in yet another revolution. The Revolution of Ayutla, rather than the usual barracks revolt, was the product of a maturing generation, born since independence, nurtured under the liberal Constitution of 1824, and eager to bring democracy and stability to their homeland. Two liberals, Juan Álvarez, the old *caudillo* from Guerrero who

[11] Walter P. Webb and H. Bailey Carroll (eds.), *The Handbook of Texas*, II, 729; William C. Binkley, "New Mexico and the Texan Santa Fé Expedition," *Southwestern Historical Quarterly*, XXVII (October, 1923), 99. Quote is from the *Handbook*.

[12] Roel, *Nuevo León*, 157; Circular letters signed by Vidaurri, August 14, 1843, June 25, 1844, March 17, 1845, in Western Americana Collection.

in the past forty years had participated in every antidictatorial uprising, and Ignacio Comonfort, former collector of customs for the port of Acapulco, published the *Plan de Ayutla* in March, 1854. They called for a temporary dictatorship to be followed by an election and a new constitution. The movement started slowly, with the old dictator, Antonio López de Santa Anna, clinging tenaciously to his office and hoping that he could discredit the liberals by charging them with anticlericalism. But the revolution soon gained strength when two strongmen, Santos Degollado in Jalisco and Manuel Doblado in Guanajuato, both announced support. Vidaurri took advantage of the chaotic situation throughout the country to overthrow the conservative governor of Nuevo León, General Gerónimo Cardona. Cardona, a weak ruler, appeared blind to his subordinate's plotting until the actual take-over.[13]

Vidaurri and Juan Zuazua, his brilliant military strategist, first plotted to seize Monterrey, the most important city in the north. Cardona was virtually powerless to stop the rebels because his army was insufficient for the task. He could expect no help from Santa Anna, who was then fully occupied fighting Comonfort and Álvarez in the south. Zuazua established himself in the village of Lampazos, both his and Vidaurri's birthplace, approximately ninety-five miles north of Monterrey. On May 11 Vidaurri, who was to be the political chief of the new government, joined him. Together they issued the *Plan del Restaurador de la Libertad,* also known as the Movement of Lampazos. With Vidaurri in command, the insurgents occupied strategic positions around Monterrey and captured the plaza on May 23 with only a few losses. They imprisoned, along with the commander, the entire garrison that had defended the city. Vidaurri declared himself governor and military commander; he named Zuazua colonel. Garza Ayala and Naranjo had aided Vidaurri in his conquest of Monterrey, and other liberals in Nuevo León then came to Vidaurri's aid,

---

[13] For a study of this revolution, see Richard A. Johnson, *The Mexican Revolution of Ayutla, 1854–1855: An Analysis of the Evolution and Destruction of Santa Anna's Last Dictatorship.* See also Wilfrid H. Callcott, *Church and State in Mexico, 1822–1857,* 234.

with Zaragoza pronouncing in Victoria, Escobedo and Aramberri in the southern part of the state.[14]

A victory had been won for all northerners, decreed Vidaurri. Unlike the miserable Indians of the south who had succumbed to Santa Anna's tyranny, the people of Nuevo León, he asserted, would now be guaranteed property, security, and a stable, enlightened government. Although he was in agreement with the principles of the *Plan de Ayutla*, Vidaurri pointed out that he had taken Monterrey in a separate action. Nor was his *coup* simply local in nature, for Vidaurri hoped to extend eventually the freedom and rights of the *Plan del Restaurador de la Libertad* to all the states.[15]

An efficient administrator, Vidaurri quickly stabilized his government. For years he had admired the governmental system of the United States, as did most nineteenth-century Latin Americans, and he borrowed freely from it in his effort to give Nuevo León an effective government. Assembling a group of influential citizens of Monterrey, he wisely sought their approval of his *plan*. By May 25 he had framed the *Plan de Monterrey*, a new constitution containing the essence of his states' rights philosophy. Although it preserved the existing judicial and bureaucratic organization of the state, this new constitution initiated significant changes. Nuevo León was to be independent until the nation established what Vidaurri considered a truly republican (or democratic) form of government. Even then he stipulated that each state would retain its sovereignty, thus decentralizing the federal government. The militia, for example, would be controlled locally, thus insuring that too much power would not gravitate to the federal government. This obviously was a reaction to the years of autocratic, centralist rule under Santa Anna and his conservative lieutenants and allies. To assure support from powerful local

[14] *Suplemento al número 2 del Restaurador de la Libertad* (Monterrey), June 4, 1855; Edward H. Moseley, "The Public Career of Santiago Vidaurri, 1855–1858," 71–72; Vito Alessio Robles, *Monterrey en la historia y en la leyenda*, 240–241; Roel, *Nuevo León*, 157; Naranjo, *Lampazos*, 131–133.

[15] *El Restaurador de la Libertad* (Monterrey), May 28, June 4, 1855; Moseley, "Santiago Vidaurri," 82–83.

leaders, Vidaurri established a five-member advisory council to assist him.[16]

Many other decisions had to be made. The army, taxes, and the extension of the *plan* were items requiring prompt attention. Supplying and controlling the army particularly proved to be an immediate problem. Vidaurri initially obtained munitions from traders on the Texas border. One of these was José María Jesús Carvajal, the well-known filibuster who had incited trouble along the Rio Grande for years. After capturing Monterrey, however, Vidaurri provided the arms himself in order to avoid encouraging such opportunists. He further enforced strict discipline by ordering stiff punishment for deserters and officers who allowed their men to flee.[17] Most important of all, the army had to be paid, thus leading to another perplexing difficulty–taxation.

The people of Nuevo León were neither accustomed to paying high taxes, nor could they afford them. Previous governments had been content with the customs receipts, which usually found their way into officials' pockets instead of the treasury. Vidaurri changed this. He improved the customs collections almost overnight by ordering all illegal trade goods confiscated. Then he approached the dean of the Monterrey Cathedral, José Guillermo Montemayor, and subtly but firmly suggested that the church contribute to the government–and stay out of politics. He also assigned a specific sum as the contribution from each municipality, warning that unless the taxes were raised, many men would be conscripted into the state militia and the money taken out of their salaries.[18]

When his control of Monterrey was assured, Vidaurri began to export his revolution, proving his earlier assertion that the *Plan*

[16] *El Restaurador de la Libertad* (Monterrey), June 4, 11, 30, 1855; Broadside dated May 25, in S. D. Mullowny to Secretary of State William L. Marcy, Monterrey, May 27, 1855, in Despatches From United States Consuls in Monterrey, Mexico, 1849–1906: Register, 1849–1906 and Vol. II, November 15, 1849–December 9, 1869.

[17] Moseley, "Santiago Vidaurri," 86–88; *El Restaurador de la Libertad* (Monterrey), June 18, 1855.

[18] Mullowny to Marcy, Monterrey, May 10, 1855, in Monterrey Consular Despatches; *El Restaurador de la Libertad* (Monterrey), June 4, 11, 18, 23, July 7, 1855.

de Monterrey was intended for more states than just Nuevo León. On May 25 he invited both Tamaulipas and Coahuila to join him. A single government, he indicated, could be much more effective in combatting such threats as the Indians who troubled the western and northern frontiers and the filibusters who constantly crossed the Rio Grande at Matamoros. Encouraged by the liberal governor of Tamaulipas, Juan José de la Garza, Vidaurri moved his troops against conservative General Adrían Woll in Matamoros, and Tamaulipas quickly accepted the plan. When Vidaurri learned that another conservative force under General Francisco Güitián was approaching Saltillo and would likely be on the road to Monterrey soon, he turned his army toward Saltillo and requested that General Valentín Cruz, governor and military commander of Coahuila, aid him in meeting Güitián. Thus reinforced, Vidaurri's forces met those of Güitián in July, 1855, at the Rancho de las Varas, near Saltillo. Under the leadership of Zuazua and Captain Ignacio Zaragoza, Vidaurri's troops won a decisive victory on July 23, greatly aided by several spies in Saltillo. Coahuila accepted the *plan* on July 26.[19]

Administering Coahuila was a special problem; perhaps Vidaurri was thinking already of permanently annexing it. He expanded his system—particularly customs collection—into the state, but did not yet declare its outright annexation. He proclaimed himself the military and political head of the state, but appointed a Coahuilan secretary. Because of his boyhood residence near Monclova, the former capital, Vidaurri was assured of the support of many friends, but he realized that he also had numerous enemies.[20]

The next state to be offered the *Plan de Monterrey* as a cure for all its governmental and social ills was San Luis Potosí. In August Vidaurri sent his able military strategist, Zuazua, to subordinate the region. The conservatives in San Luis, however, had other

[19] Moseley, "Santiago Vidaurri," 92–93; Gabriel Saldívar, *Historia Compendiada de Tamaulipas,* 206–207; Flores Tapia, *Coahuila,* 21; Roel, *Nuevo León,* 158; *Texas State Times* (Austin), August 25, 1855; Guillermo Colín Sánchez, *Ignacio Zaragoza, evocación de un héroe,* 28–29.

[20] Moseley, "Santiago Vidaurri," 100–110; *Boletín Extraordinario* (Monterrey), supplement to *El Restaurador de la Libertad* (Monterrey), July 24, 1855.

plans. They were already preparing to accept the *Plan de Ayutla,* about as much concession as they cared to make. They hoped that conservatives would be able to influence the national government, therefore making Ayutla preferable to Vidaurri's domination. Vidaurri unsuccessfully protested to President Álvarez, who had seized power as revolutionary chief when Santa Anna fled, that many of the officials of that state were those previously expelled from Tamaulipas; these former tyrants, he insisted, should not be admitted into the revolution.[21] This probably was the first such objection that Vidaurri raised, indicating that he wanted a free hand in the north. Actually he feared that admission of San Luis Potosí to the *plan* of Álvarez would have been a move toward centralized government, that is, expansion of the central government into the north, and therefore an invasion of his domain.[22] The same "tyrants" would have been welcomed to the *Plan de Monterrey.*

The national reaction to Vidaurri's seizure in Nuevo León varied. The rapid spread of his influence in the north immediately stimulated rumors that he would establish an independent republic comprising the three border states of Nuevo León, Coahuila, and Tamaulipas. Santa Anna, recalling the numerous attempts during the past two decades to establish a republic in the north, charged that Vidaurri had seized power in Nuevo León as a part of another American filibuster attempt. Renewing an old and almost traditional charge against northern *caudillos,* Santa Anna insisted that this was the beginning of the Republic of Sierra Madre (the name most often suggested for the proposed northern republic). In fact, the charge might have had some substance. Texas slaveholders had contacted Vidaurri immediately after his victory requesting that he found a republic in northern Mexico to

---

[21] *Boletín Oficial* (Monterrey), August 19, September 28, 1855; Primo Feliciano Velázquez, *Historia de San Luis Potosí,* III, 270–271. Vidaurri changed the name of the official state newspaper from *El Restaurador de la Libertad* to *Boletín Oficial.* Although the name of the official government gazette of Nuevo León frequently changed, all the papers used for this research are available on the same microfilm series from the Library of Congress. The copy used for this research is in the Texas Christian University Library.

[22] Moseley, "Santiago Vidaurri," 140.

serve as a buffer zone between slave territory and free territory which would enable them to retrieve their fugitive slaves who had sought freedom in Mexico.[23] The fact that Vidaurri's revolution was independent of Comonfort's and Álvarez's only added to the impression that the northern *caudillo* was indeed seeking independence.[24]

Most liberals, however, were willing to welcome Vidaurri into their movement, preferring not to denounce so powerful a governor without absolute proof that he was disloyal. Some felt uneasy about Vidaurri's friendship, because the charges of Santa Anna were by no means groundless. Vidaurri had been gathering arms, ammunition, and horses in the north. Álvarez privately suspected him of preparing to enlist filibuster support from the United States, either to enforce his demands against the federal government or to declare his independence from Mexico. But the *puros,* the extreme liberals, considered Vidaurri one of them.[25] Guillermo Prieto, Álvarez's minister of the treasury, wrote Manuel Doblado,

[23] Johnson, *Ayutla,* 60, quoting Santa Anna's charges in the *Diario Oficial* (Mexico City); Ronnie C. Tyler, "The Callahan Expedition of 1855: Indians or Negroes?" *Southwestern Historical Quarterly,* LXX (April, 1967), 578.

[24] Siliceo to Manuel Doblado, México, September 3, 1855, in Genaro García (ed.), *Documentos inéditos o muy raros para la historia de México,* XXVI, 138–141. Oscar Flores Tapia feels that Vidaurri intended to establish such a republic. In fact, he quotes from a letter, supposedly from Vidaurri to Zuazua, in which Vidaurri wrote: "Basta de charla Juan; cuando estoy de vena corre me pluma con la rapidez de una bala Sharp: la toma de San Luis me tiene loco de gusto. Ésta plaza interesante me va a servir para establecer la república de la Sierra Madre, si llega el remoto caso en que triunfen los puros de oriente de los puros del norte." (Enough chatting, Juan; when I am inspired my pen runs with the speed of a Sharp bullet: the capture of San Luis has made me crazy with pleasure. This interesting place will serve to establish the Republic of Sierra Madre, if the remote chance that the *puros* of the east triumph over the *puros* of the north happens.") The letter is dated July 12, 1858, although Flores Tapia gives no reference, and no record of it can be found in the Vidaurri-Zuazua correspondence in the Archivo General del Estado de Nuevo León. See Flores Tapia, *Coahuila,* 23.

[25] All the liberals supported the program of reform, but the moderates thought the program should be implemented slowly, and the *puros* thought it "could and should be done suddenly." Justo Sierra, *Juárez, su obra y su tiempo,* 90. See also Callcott, *Church and State,* 241; Johnson, *Ayutla,* 111.

governor of Guanajuato, "I can assure you that the doctrines of Vidaurri have an eminent place in the *puro* party."[26]

Vidaurri helped his own cause immensely by responding vigorously to a Texan invasion, then claiming that he had thus proved his loyalty to Mexico and to liberal principles. In October, 1855, Captain James Hughes Callahan, a veteran Indian fighter, led over 100 Texas Rangers into Coahuila for the expressed purpose of punishing marauding Indians.[27] The Texans were led into Mexico for additional reasons, but foremost among them was the hope that Vidaurri would accept their support, declare his independence from Mexico, and establish a republic in the north. They, in fact, had offered him 1,000 armed and mounted men to aid in such a venture, but Vidaurri had refused them. Vidaurri realized that their real aim was to recover fugitive slaves and instructed his officers to "repel force with force." The invaders were easily turned back. He then sent hundreds of troops and several pieces of artillery to the border to prevent a second invasion.[28] When news of this incident reached Mexico City, the *puros* rejoiced. They felt Vidaurri had proved himself a loyal son of the liberal movement.[29]

Now convinced of Vidaurri's trustworthiness, President Álvarez allowed him to participate in the organization of the new government. Álvarez, in fact, was so relieved that he did not have Vidaurri as an enemy that he allowed the governor *de facto* jurisdiction over the neighboring state of Coahuila, although legal annexation was not granted. For his part, Vidaurri supported the *Plan de Ayutla* nationally, but stipulated that he must be allowed to govern

[26] Prieto to Doblado, México, September 5, 1855, in García, *Documentos inéditos*, XXVI, 144–146.

[27] Ernest Shearer, "The Callahan Expedition, 1855," *Southwestern Historical Quarterly*, LIV (April, 1951), 430–431.

[28] Broadside (no title, n.d., signed in ink by Hanson Alsbury). Original in the Santiago Roel Papers; Mullowny to Marcy, Monterrey, October 23, 1855, in Monterrey Consular Despatches; *Daily National Intelligencer* (Washington, D.C.), November 13, 1855. Quote is in *El Siglo Diez y Nueve* (México), November 8, 1855, and *Boletín Oficial* (Monterrey), October 24, 1855.

[29] Johnson, *Ayutla*, 111; Vicente Riva Palacio, *México a través de los siglos*, V, 82.

Nuevo León and Coahuila according to his own *Plan de Monter-rey*.[30]

Vidaurri's victory also strengthened his internal control over the north. Because of his vigorous action to defend the frontier, the people of Nuevo León enthusiastically supported him. Although he still had some enemies in Coahuila, a stronger faction stood behind him.[31] Opposition in Tamaulipas was so chaotic that effective resistance, or even a self-enforced maintenance of peace within its borders, was impossible, and he was able to use the extended powers on the frontier, awarded him by Álvarez, to gain control of that state. First Vidaurri collected the customs duties in Tamaulipas, then further extended his control of the state at the expense of Governor Garza, even though that statesman was a liberal.[32] Garza would no longer be a potential threat to Vidaurri's control of the north.[33]

Inspired by a sense of destiny and a desire to unite the northern states under one government, Vidaurri moved a larger portion of his army into Tamaulipas in November. This indiscretion produced two unfortunate results for him: it clearly showed his designing nature, and it ended in failure. When Vidaurri began the conquest, Garza unleashed a propaganda barrage from Matamoros, through broadsides and the official state newspaper, which soon bore results. Repeating charges that Vidaurri wanted to form the Republic of Sierra Madre, he effectively undermined the invader's popularity in Tamaulipas and, temporarily, in Nuevo León. Vidaurri also faced the usual tactical problems confronting every advancing army. He overextended himself. Bad roads created an impossible supply problem. Indian raids and filibuster threats—the thinly spread U.S. Army could not patrol the entire border—in the neighboring state of Coahuila, which Vidaurri now claimed to

[30] Johnson, *Ayutla*, 111; Moseley, "Santiago Vidaurri," 160–163; *Boletín Oficial* (Monterrey), October 26, 1855.

[31] Moseley, "Santiago Vidaurri," 162–167; U.S. Congress, *Senate Executive Documents*, 45th Cong., 2nd Sess., Document No. 19, p. 110.

[32] *Boletín Oficial* (Monterrey), October 26, 1855; *El Restaurador de la Libertad* (Monterrey), November 13, 1855.

[33] Moseley, "Santiago Vidaurri," 169–172.

have legally annexed, simultaneously emphasized the fact that he should be on the defensive in his own state. Because the state treasury suffered from both dishonest customs officials and a decline in international trade after the Callahan affair, local grumbling grew louder. If this were not enough, the federal government remained neutral, preferring to support whichever side could bring peace and maintain order. In December, 1855, when President Comonfort, who had recently replaced the elderly Álvarez, recognized Garza as the legitimate governor of the state, Vidaurri had to stop his aggression.[34]

Many thought that this debacle would break Vidaurri's domination of the north, for no sooner had he returned from Tamaulipas than he learned that Comonfort had refused to recognize the legality of his annexation of Coahuila. The final decision, however, rested with a committee from the Constitutional Congress that had been legally assembled under a provision in the *Plan de Ayutla*. The committee, after studying the question, reported on May 26, 1856, that the people of Coahuila should be allowed to decide their own fate. This seemed to please everyone except Vidaurri, who insisted that the Coahuilans had already chosen, then moved to strengthen his grasp on the territory, making it increasingly clear that he would not be deprived of the land.[35]

Despairing of a solution to the impasse, Comonfort ordered Vidaurri to surrender his governorship to José de Jesús Dávila y Prieto, former Nuevo León chief executive, until the problem could be resolved.[36] When Vidaurri refused, Comonfort sent General Vicente Rosas Landa to enforce the decision of the federal government. Instead of fighting, however, Rosas Landa and Vidaurri agreed to talk and soon reached a solution by negotiating a

[34] Ibid., 180–181; *El Restaurador de la Libertad* (Monterrey), November 20, 1855; *Boletín Oficial* (Monterrey), November 21, 1855.
[35] Moseley, "Santiago Vidaurri," 193, 204, 207–208; Edward H. Moseley, "Santiago Vidaurri, Champion of States' Rights: 1855–1857," *West Georgia College Studies in the Social Sciences*, VI (June, 1967), 76; Flores Tapia, *Coahuila*, 24–28.
[36] Federico Berrueto Ramón, "Santiago Vidaurri y el estado de Nuevo León y Coahuila," *Humánitas*, VI (1965), 407–420; Moseley, "Vidaurri, Champion of States' Rights," 77–79; Roel, *Nuevo León*, 136.

treaty, on November 18, which stipulated that Nuevo León and Coahuila would be governed by a council of state until the Coahuilans could decide for themselves who would be their ruler.[37] The discussion took place on the floor of the Coahuilan congress, with delegates speaking for and against the plan to unite the two states. The deputy from Monclova, Miguel Blanco, a Vidaurri supporter, claimed that there was historical precedent for such a union because Miguel Ramos Arizpe, the author of the Constitution of 1824, had proposed a union between Nuevo León, Coahuila, and Tamaulipas in 1812. There was some opposition, but not sufficient to prevent the union, apparently because some of the delegates feared Vidaurri. Not only did he still have great influence in the state, but he also had the most powerful army in the north.[38] Nuevo León and Coahuila were now legally united.

Vidaurri's maintenance of control in Coahuila meant that he had cleared a major hurdle in his bid for regional power; he had successfully defied the federal government, gaining all the respect and self-confidence that accompanies a cherished victory. Fearing that further conflict would split the liberals and catapult the conservatives into power, the national congress submitted in late 1856 by allowing Vidaurri legally to annex Coahuila.[39] Perhaps Coahuila was a bribe to keep the most powerful man on the frontier in the liberal camp.

Soon Vidaurri became the leader of a liberal army so strong that he could greatly influence national politics. In January, 1857, he left Juan Nepomuceno de la Garza y Evia, a lawyer and former state executive, as interim governor and personally took command of the Nuevo León army, already one of the best in Mexico.[40] On January 22 he marched on San Luis Potosí, determined to subjugate the state. He easily captured the city and his prestige

[37] *Boletín Oficial* (Monterrey), November 22, 1855.
[38] Niceto de Zamaçois, *Historia de Méjico*, XIV, 342–343; *El Restaurador de la Libertad* (Monterrey), March 13, 1857; Flores Tapia, *Coahuila*, 38–40; Riva Palacio, *México*, V, 195.
[39] Flores Tapia, *Coahuila*, 40.
[40] *El Restaurador de la Libertad* (Monterrey), February 6, 1857; Roel, *Nuevo León*, 131–132, 165–166; Charles Lempriere, *Notes in Mexico in 1861 and 1862: Politically and Socially Considered*, 274.

soared. Álvarez dubbed him a "son of the liberal movement," and
he seemed more an ally of President Comonfort than a subordinate.[41]

Once Vidaurri had secured his personal position, he turned his
attention to resolving the usual problems of a nineteenth-century
frontier chief: rustlers, American and Mexican; Indians, especially
the Lipan Apaches and Comanches who raided into Texas and
then sought refuge in Mexico and vice versa; insufficient resources, financial and material; and, on at least one occasion, a
smallpox epidemic. His responses to these problems provided other
leaders with guidelines. To meet the Indian problem, he strengthened the frontier defenses, working out an arrangement for cooperation between the northern Mexican states and the United
States.[42] Vidaurri attempted to organize the more "peaceful" tribes
to act as a buffer on the frontier. The government concluded
treaties with various tribes, granting them land in return for service in the militia. In response to a threatening smallpox epidemic,
Vidaurri actively encouraged the use of the smallpox vaccine, which
effectively checked the spread of the disease.[43]

Generally Vidaurri's was a popular and progressive government.
Certain facets of his administration reflected liberal policies. In
August, 1857, a revised Nuevo León y Coahuila constitution out-
lawed slavery. By providing that anyone entering the state was

[41] Zamaçois, *Historia de Méjico*, XIV, 437; *El Restaurador de la Libertad*
(Monterrey), February 6, 1857; *Segundo Boletín Oficial Extraordinario*
(Monterrey), February 17, 1857. The *Segundo Boletín* was issued as a supplement to the official newspaper. Quote is from Moseley, "Santiago Vidaurri,"
261–262.

[42] *El Restaurador de la Libertad* (Monterrey), January 23, 30, February 6,
April 10, October 30, November 13, 1857. See Kenneth W. Porter, "The
Seminole in Mexico, 1850–1861," *Hispanic American Historical Review*, XXXI
(February, 1951), 1–36; Odie B. Faulk (ed.), "Projected Mexican Colonies
in the Borderlands, 1852," *Journal of Arizona History*, X (Summer, 1969),
115–128.

[43] Edward H. Moseley, "Indians From the Eastern United States and the
Defense of Northeastern Mexico: 1855–1864," *Southwestern Social Science
Quarterly*, LXVI (December, 1965), 273–280; Porter, "Seminole in Mexico,"
1–36; *El Restaurador de la Libertad* (Monterrey), February 6, 1857; Ken-
neth W. Porter, "Wild Cat's Death and Burial," *Chronicles of Oklahoma*,
XXI (March, 1943), 41–43.

free, it encouraged many Negroes to risk their lives to gain refuge in Mexico. This provision, however, was a source of difficulty in later negotiations with the Confederate States. The constitution expanded the right of suffrage; anyone who had lived in the state for a year and was making an "honest" living could vote. The document also provided for a gubernatorial election every two years. Other features included the assignment of budget control to the legislators and a stipulation that no soldier or national officer could be governor.[44]

Vidaurri's domestic program was quite effective. He began a program of beautification and encouraged the development of the theater and arts. Another important part of his domestic policy centered on education. He instigated legislation for the creation of the Colegio Civil, an institution still in operation. To improve administrative efficiency further, he divided the state of Nuevo León y Coahuila into ten *cantones*, or regions, and in addition set up a plan to liquidate the state debt.[45]

Because Nuevo León could profit from an active business community, Vidaurri initiated a program of international trade and encouraged all businessmen. He engaged in commerce himself with his son-in-law, Patricio Milmo, and assisted others in founding La Fama, a textile factory in nearby Santa Catarina. Railroads, he believed, were necessary if the area were to continue advancing.[46] Business and manufacturing made considerable headway

[44] *El Restaurador de la Libertad* (Monterrey), August 21, 1857, contains a copy of the new constitution.

[45] Roel, *Nuevo León*, 166, 168–169, 174–175; *El Restaurador de la Libertad* (Monterrey), November 13, 1857; Israel Cavazos Garza, *El Colegio Civil de Nuevo León: para su historia.*

[46] *El Restaurador de la Libertad* (Monterrey), September 4, 1857; Roel, *Nuevo León*, 166; Moseley, "Santiago Vidaurri," 305. By the time Vidaurri associated himself with Milmo in business, Milmo already was a successful merchant and trader who had journeyed to Mexico in 1848. He arrived in Tampico, but proceeded immediately to San Luis Postosí and went to work for his uncle, James Milmo, who owned an importing house there. He soon established his own importing house in both Monterrey and Matamoros. Patricio Milmo was a member of an old and respected Irish family that settled in Sligo in the sixteenth century. His given name was Patrick, but it was changed through usage to Patricio. See the New York *Times,* February 18, 1899, p. 7; the New York *Herald,* February 17,

under Vidaurri and indeed established the firm foundation that allowed Monterrey to become the industrial giant of Mexico to-day.[47]

By 1857, when the nation further disintegrated in the War of the Reform, Vidaurri had eliminated practically all active opposition in his realm and was securely in control. The War of the Reform, or the Three Years' War, was, in a sense, a continuation of the Revolution of Ayutla. The liberals, or federalists, were still pitted against the conservatives, or centralists. In this sense, then, the war was one of the provinces against Mexico City. But it was more, for it was a guerrilla war, a war of the country against the town, an all-out battle to decide finally whether the nation would be dominated by the pure-blood Spanish/church faction or by the creole (native-born) anticlerical faction.[48]

With his first goal—self-preservation—secure, Vidaurri could give attention to his second—his constituents—even during the brutal civil war. By negotiating with the clergy he softened the blows of the Ley Juárez and the Ley Lerdo, two laws which stripped the church of much of its power, but harmony did not long endure. Bishop Francisco de Paula Verea, unwilling to compromise his position, refused to administer the sacraments to government officials. When it became obvious that Bishop Paula Verea would not cooperate, Vidaurri called a meeting of influential citizens, arrested the cleric, and expelled him from the state. The other members of the clergy, faced with the bishop's fate, rescinded their decision and once again administered the sacraments to the members of the government.[49]

The confusion resulting from Félix Zuloaga's announcement of

18, 1899, pp. 12, 13, respectively; copy of a clipping from the New York *Tribune* (undated), in possession of Sra. Berta Zambrano de Milmo, Monterrey; the *Daily Express* (San Antonio), February 16, 1899, p. 5.

[47] Isidro Vizcaya Canales, *Los orígenes de la industrialización de Monterrey (1867–1920)*, xix-xx; Horacio Garduño García, *Nuevo León, un ejemplo de protección a la industria de transformación*, 39.

[48] See Walter V. Scholes, *Mexican Politics During the Juárez Regime, 1855–1872*, 25–42.

[49] *El Restaurador de la Libertad* (Monterrey), August 28, September 11, 25, November 6, 1857; *Boletín Oficial* (Monterrey), September 9, 1857.

his *Plan de Tacubaya* in December, 1857, allowed Vidaurri to strengthen further his hold on the northern states. When the congress convened in the fall of 1857, President Comonfort requested extraordinary powers, even before he named his cabinet. Fearful that he would betray the liberal cause by nominating still-powerful conservatives to the cabinet, the congress refused to grant the request. Zuloaga pronounced on behalf of Comonfort and the conservative faction, stipulating that Comonfort should be given the dictatorial powers, the Constitution of 1857 should be revoked, and a new constituent assembly should be elected. Comonfort hesitated, hoping that he could hold the country together, but the conservatives refused to be put off. Zuloaga issued another *pronunciamiento* in January, 1858, removing Comonfort from office. When it became evident that his troops could not control the city, Comonfort went into exile, leaving Zuloaga and the conservatives in control of the capital. As far as the liberals were concerned, Benito Juárez, the president of the supreme court and the first in the line of presidential succession, was now the legal president.[50]

Apparently remaining loyal to the liberals, Vidaurri helped Juárez. But Vidaurri requested that Juárez not send troops into his own two states, for the governor stated that no federal control would be required in Nuevo León y Coahuila. When the clergy, hoping to secure repeal of the reform laws, accepted Zuloaga's proposal in January, Vidaurri expelled them from Monterrey, then used this "betrayal" and other excuses to extract a legislative mandate on January 19, giving him special powers until the basic law of the land–the Constitution of 1857–could be re-instituted.[51] Declaring the independence of Nuevo León y Coahuila, he vested judicial supremacy in the state courts. As one of the first liberals to enforce the *Ley Lerdo,* which forced the church to sell its large estates to anyone with enough money to purchase them, he further increased his popularity among anticlerical classes. But he also

[50] *Boletín Oficial* (Monterrey), December 29, 1857; Broadside (supplement to the official paper), December 31, 1857.

[51] *Boletín Oficial* (Monterrey), January 10, 23, 1858; Ricardo Lancaster-Jones, "Don Francisco de Paula Verea, Obispo de Linares y de Puebla," *Humánitas,* VII (1966), 403–404.

31

issued a decree calling for death to anyone who disrupted the order of the state.[52] Clearly working to concentrate his power, Vidaurri used national laws when they suited his purpose; when they did not, he made his own. The same dictatorial methods which he so roundly denounced in other administrations could, it seemed, be justified in his own.

Conservative opposition to Vidaurri in the north again centered in San Luis Potosí, where the effort was more costly this time. In March President Juárez ordered Vidaurri to take the city, but the *caudillo* stalled when Zuazua, his trusted military chief, predicted almost certain defeat. By his refusal to attack at the President's order, Vidaurri hampered the national effort and proved once again that he cared more for his own state than for the nation. After a short pause, however, Vidaurri moved against San Luis Potosí, capturing it in July. Zuazua continued until he had also brought Guanajuato under liberal domination. And in August Vidaurri appointed the president of the Nuevo León supreme court as acting governor and went into the field himself. By September, 1858, he was probably the most powerful liberal in Mexico; more than 7,500 of his *norteños* had won a series of victories under his direction and new recruits arrived daily. Even Americans such as Sheriff William R. Henry of Bexar County, Texas, and Colonel Samuel A. Lockridge, both rather infamous filibusters who had frequently invaded Mexico with volunteers seeking personal gain, offered to join the *caudillo*.[53] Never was Vidaurri more powerful or influential.

The conservatives renewed their propaganda campaign against him, this time revealing new weapons in their arsenal of charges with amazing results. Not only did he certainly plan to establish the Republic of Sierra Madre with American help, they charged, but also his conflicts with the church demonstrated a desire to establish Greek paganism as the national religion. Anti-Catholicism was a charge frequently hurled against the reformers by the con-

---

[52] *Boletín Oficial* (Monterrey), January 31, 1858.

[53] Ibid., March 18, July 5, 1858; Moseley, "Santiago Vidaurri," 329–330, 346–347, 350; Henry to Vidaurri, San Antonio, June 13, 1858, and Vidaurri to Henry, Monterrey, July 12, 1858, in Expediente 437, Correspondencia Particular de Don Santiago Vidaurri.

servatives. And then by committing atrocities of war in San Luis Potosí, Vidaurri's own troops made him vulnerable to the vocal, more truthful accusations of brutality from the frightened citizenry.[54]

Convinced that maintaining San Luis Potosí was more trouble than it was worth, Vidaurri prepared to withdraw his troops on September 11. Again, keeping his army adequately supplied proved a serious problem. Perhaps even worse, the citizens of Nuevo León, usually enthusiastic supporters of his programs, began to grumble about the high war taxes. Payments soon faltered. As if he needed any more persuasion to convince him to retreat, Vidaurri apprehensively watched some 5,000 conservative troops under General Miguel Miramón advance.[55]

Vidaurri marched a short distance from San Luis Potosí, establishing his headquarters near the village of Ahualulco, approximately thirty-five miles northwest of the city. Zuazua was not content with this defensive position and wanted to move. In an action never fully explained and unanimously condemned by observers as a mistake, Vidaurri removed Zuazua, the man on whom he had depended for military advice and leadership since his first victory in 1855, and appointed an American soldier of fortune, Edward H. Jordan, to replace him.[56] Miramón advanced, met the liberal forces on September 29, and routed them.[57] Although he blamed the setback on poor equipment, no protection from the elements, and sabotage of his artillery, Vidaurri publicly admitted to the people of Nuevo León y Coahuila that he had suffered a stunning defeat. He withdrew his troops and escaped to Monterrey, but he never again wielded such strong national influence.[58]

---

[54] *Boletín Oficial* (Monterrey), August 21, 1858; Zamaçois, *Historia de Méjico*, XV, 29; Velázquez, *Historia de San Luis Potosí*, III, 297–306.

[55] Velázquez, *Historia de San Luis Potosí*, III, 306; Moseley, "Santiago Vidaurri," 354–357.

[56] Velázquez, *Historia de San Luis Potosí*, III, 306–307; Roel, *Nuevo León*, 160; Naranjo, *Lampazos*, 147–148.

[57] *Boletín Oficial* (Monterrey), October 26, 1858; Velázquez, *Historia de San Luis Potosí*, III, 308–309.

[58] Velázquez, *Historia de San Luis Potosí*, III, 317; Moseley, "Santiago Vidaurri," 360.

The defeat at Ahualulco was one of the turning points in Vidaurri's career. During the hectic years of the War of the Reform, his control of the north was threatened from both sides. Should the conservatives win they would render the state subject to the national government as a matter of course. For the liberals to win, however, Vidaurri would have to place the national effort ahead of his own power and desires for northern Mexico. This he refused to do. When the fears of federal intervention into the north became reality, Vidaurri thought only of himself. In a war of desperation that prostrated the country, a war that was ultimately won by the liberals only because of the tenacity and dedication of their leaders, Vidaurri deserted both Juárez and the liberal cause –all because his domain was seriously threatened.[59]

With his drive toward national prominence blunted, Vidaurri began to reinforce his position in Monterrey. He still realized that he had to rely on trade and customs revenues for prosperity. Consequently, he probably seriously reconsidered the possibility of establishing a republic that would be free from the trade restrictions and the demands of tax money and manpower that came from a government struggling for survival. In an effort to draw nearer to Texas, both commercially and politically, he offered Governor Hardin R. Runnels an extradition treaty that would include the return of slaves who had fled to Mexico to gain their freedom, something that the state's slave owners had desired for years. He proposed that Nuevo León y Coahuila and Texas conclude such a pact, since none existed between the United States and Mexico and none was likely; abolitionist pressure in the United States as well as the liberal constitution of Mexico stipulated that slaves, upon entering Mexico, became free men. (Governor Runnels, of course, had to refuse, because the United States Constitution forbids a state to make a treaty with a foreign state or nation.)[60] After the American Civil War began, Vidaurri considered an alliance with the South, indicating the length to which he would go

---

[59] Moseley, "Santiago Vidaurri," 360, also considers this a turning point in Vidaurri's career.

[60] Juan N. Seguín to Hardin R. Runnels, San Antonio, January 9, 1859, in Governors' Letters.

to defend his realm and underscoring the strength of his conviction, at least during times of trial, that the future of his state depended upon the international trade.

Although Vidaurri favored the reform laws of 1859–separation of church and state; secularization of clergy and abolition of the monasteries, brotherhoods, and other similar organizations; abolition of novitiates in convents; nationalization of all the wealth administered by clergy; elimination of the civil authority in payment of church fees–he soon split with the liberals over use of the Nuevo León militia. Restored to his post and to Vidaurri's confidence following Jordan's defeat at the battle of Ahualulco, Zuazua disputed with the governors of Aguascalientes and Zacatecas. The two men had offered asylum to Colonel Julián Quiroga, an officer who had disobeyed orders whom Zuazua was trying to punish (and, who, ironically, was considered by many an illegitimate son of Vidaurri). Zuazua even accused the governors of supporting Quiroga's disobedience. The dispute meant that any cooperation, however little, that might have been forthcoming was disrupted. On August 8 Jesús González Ortega, one of the leading liberal generals, begged Vidaurri to end the matter because it was disrupting the liberal offensive in the area. Either disgusted with the entire affair or fearing federal intervention in his domain, Vidaurri ordered the elite Nuevo León troops home.[61]

But other liberal leaders challenged Vidaurri's authority. Santos Degollado, commander of the liberal Army of the West, entered the fray on August 13 by ordering the troops to return to their positions. The soldiers hesitated momentarily, afraid to defy Degollado, but General Zuazua continued to Monterrey, where he sought the protection of Vidaurri. Vidaurri then attempted to convince the other northerners–Aramberri, Escobedo, and Zaragoza–to return as well, insisting that the Indian menace on the frontier had worsened considerably. This dispute, which greatly weakened the liberal forces, probably enabled the conservatives under General Adrián Woll to defeat General Degollado on August 30, 1859. Degollado, at any rate, was convinced of Vidaurri's dis-

[61] *Boletín Oficial* (Monterrey), September 7, 1859; Riva Palacio, *México*, V, 383–386; Roel, *Nuevo León*, 160–162; Scholes, *Mexican Politics*, 44.

loyalty and issued a decree on September 11 stripping the *caudillo* of his military and political power and ordering him to answer for his "crimes" in court. Aramberri was to act as governor of Nuevo León y Coahuila until the legislature could name a successor.[62]

While Vidaurri stalled, his followers began to choose sides. Zuazua and Quiroga supported him, lending credence to the oft-repeated rumor that Quiroga was indeed Vidaurri's son, while Aramberri, Zaragoza, Escobedo, Garza Ayala, Naranjo, José María Treviño Garza, and Pedro Martínez followed Degollado. With the federal government opposing him, Vidaurri prepared to fight the national government for at least the second time in his career, not because of any insoluable doctrinal differences, but over who would wield power in the north. Zuazua left Monterrey searching for recruits while the militarily naive Vidaurri guarded the capital. Immediately the patriots under Zaragoza pronounced against Vidaurri. They arrested him on September 25, despite the fact that he still had a military force, and named Aramberri governor. When he was released, Vidaurri went into a brief Texas exile for about two weeks.[63]

While in Texas, he made several contacts who would be extremely useful in the coming years. He met José Agustín Quintero, who later represented the Confederate States in Monterrey.[64] He also got another look at Texas and Texans–he had been in the Republic on a spy mission for General Arista–and realized that his goals and aspirations for Nuevo León y Coahuila more nearly resembled those of Texas than southern or central Mexico.

[62] *Boletín Oficial* (Monterrey), September 20, 26, 1859; letters of Degollado in Ernesto de la Torre Villar (ed.), *El triunfo de la república liberal, 1857–1860*, 126–130; Vicente Fuentes Díaz, *Santos Degollado, el santo de la reforma*, 110–113.

[63] *Boletín Oficial* (Monterrey), September 26, 1859; Roel, *Nuevo León*, 161–162; Riva Palacio, *México*, V, 286.

[64] Some confusion developed concerning Quintero's given name when the indexers of the *Official Records of the War of the Rebellion* erroneously listed him as "Juan." This mistake was perpetuated by a number of historians. However, W. E. Bard listed his name correctly in Webb and Carroll, *Handbook of Texas*, II, 424, as did José Manuel Carbonell, *Las poetas de "El Laud del Desterrado,"* 18, and [José Elías Hernández], *El Laud del Desterrado*, index.

Vidaurri soon returned to Nuevo León where he met Zuazua in Lampazos, the site of their first bid for power, to lay plans for recovering Monterrey. Negotiating with the interim officials through Zuazua, Vidaurri was able to complete arrangements for a new election. The victory of a Vidaurri supporter, Domingo Martínez, marked the beginning of the *caudillo's* restoration. In a second referendum, some three months later, Vidaurri's name was on the ballot, but he did not receive a majority. He got only about 8,000 out of 19,000 votes cast, so the state legislature made the choice. Vidaurri still had sufficient support in the legislature to reclaim his office.[65]

Not everyone willingly accepted the outcome. Some members of the legislature were considerably upset and influenced that body to repeal its January 19, 1855, resolution, which gave Vidaurri dictatorial powers. He responded by dissolving the legislature. This rift, however, was more serious than the previous ones. Now in open rebellion, the dissident legislators met in Galeana, approximately fifty miles south of Monterrey, where they were supported by both Aramberri and Escobedo.[66]

Because of his policy of establishing and maintaining a National Guard, Vidaurri retained firm control of the state government. The Guard was well trained and mobile.[67] He could still inspire the men, for they continued to respect him. Fully expecting that Zuazua would quell the uprising in short order, he sent the general against the "rump" legislature. General Zuazua, however, never fulfilled the mission. While on the road to Saltillo, he was ambushed and killed by a group of *aramberrista* guerrillas led by Lieutenant Colonel Eugenio García.[68] Vidaurri claimed that his general had been murdered, but the rebels contended that he was

---

[65] *La Voz de la Frontera* (Monterrey), January 1, 12, March 1, 29, April 4, 1860; Roel, *Nuevo León*, 162–163; *Fort Brown Flag* (Brownsville), quoted in the *Daily Picayune* (New Orleans), August 7, 1860. *La Voz de la Frontera* was the name of the official newspaper of Nuevo León while Martínez was governor.

[66] Roel, *Nuevo León*, 163–174; *Boletín Oficial* (Monterrey), July 9, 10, 1860.

[67] Roel, *Nuevo León*, 165.

[68] Ibid., 164; *Boletín Oficial* (Monterrey), September 8, 1860.

a casualty of war. Whatever the case, Vidaurri had lost his best military leader. Even Zuazua's death, however, did not shake the *caudillo's* hold on the north. Vidaurri's strong army and efficient administration enabled him to defeat the guerrillas. Zaragoza, Aramberri, Escobedo, and several others left for Mexico City, where they joined President Juárez to continue the struggle against the conservatives, and they now considered Vidaurri a conservative.

Vidaurri emerged from the War of the Reform seemingly as strong as ever. Although deserted by the young liberals, he still possessed the winning characteristics and administrative ability that had endeared him to his constituents. He was a true citizen of the north, one who understood his countrymen and inspired them to extraordinary performances. Few travelers could comment on Vidaurri or his government without mentioning his *machismo*. He "looked like a judge rather than a soldier," claimed José Luis Blasio, who later served as Emperor Maximilian's secretary. A big man, tall, robust, with a strong, square chin, dispassionate eyes, and distinctly Indian, or perhaps Basque, features, he radiated courage. In a country that valued manliness highly, Vidaurri exhibited strength.[69]

Yet he also encouraged confidence by his kind and attentive manner. His people believed in and trusted him. Vidaurri's government was almost a family affair, with the governor confiding even what seemed to be state secrets in the populace. When he did not read a dispatch from the steps of the palace, which was his custom, it usually appeared in the official state newspaper within a few days for all to read.[70] Vidaurri's personal correspondence was voluminous, for any citizen could elicit a response from Don Santiago.

Vidaurri was one of a generation of young northerners who loved the north, but he was less willing than the others to sacrifice that

[69] José Luis Blasio, *Maximilian, Emperor of Mexico: Memoirs of His Private Secretary*, trans. and ed. by Robert Hammond Murray, 131; Viola Ann Greer, "Santiago Vidaurri, Cacique of Northern Mexico: His Relationship to Benito Juárez," 5.

[70] Joseph Walsh to Secretary of State Lewis Cass, January 11, 1858, in Monterrey Consular Despatches.

devotion to the national cause.[71] He eventually became one of the leading states' rights spokesmen in Mexico, his desire for local autonomy causing him to forsake Mexican nationalism. Party, state, and country were all subordinated to his personal interests. And in this he remained consistent. Although sometimes forced to change several of his plans rather quickly because of a military defeat or foreign threat, he always guarded his own position first and that of the people of Nuevo León second. If it was a consideration at all, the nation, or the federal government, ranked third at best.

But Vidaurri was a political and economic liberal, an advocate of states' rights, economic reforms, and many other goals of nineteenth-century thinkers. Nineteenth-century liberals generally must be classified as either political or economic liberals; not always do the two go together. Because Vidaurri evinced qualities of both during his tenure as governor, he cannot be limited to one classification or the other. He favored federalism and looked to the United States for governmental as well as social values—a characteristic of Mexico's liberal politicians.

Economically he also fits the definition. Probably because of his peculiar situation on the frontier—that is, trade with Texas was easier and undoubtedly more profitable than exchange with the interior of Mexico—he believed in individual initiative and an economy free from government interference. If Nuevo León was to be prosperous, Vidaurri had to have a free hand in commerce. He opposed the primary monopoly of the day, the church, presumably for the same reason.[72]

It is apparent, however, that the loss of Zuazua affected Vidaurri's later career. Perhaps his own lack of military knowledge ultimately forced Vidaurri to desert the Juárez regime completely and support the French during the intervention.[73] With Zuazua

---

[71] Manuel Neira Barragán, "El folklore en el noreste de México durante la intervención francesa," in Ángel Basols Batalla et al, *Temas y figuras de la intervención*, 36.
[72] Charles A. Hale, *Mexican Liberalism in the Age of Mora, 1821–1853*, 209, 249.
[73] Roel, *Nuevo León*, 165; Naranjo, *Lampazos*, 120.

he could depend upon the *norteños* themselves to preserve his control of Nuevo León y Coahuila, but without the general he would have to depend upon diplomacy and foreign help. He could not involve himself in either of these without compromising Mexican nationalism and establishing what amounted to an independent government in Monterrey.

CHAPTER II

VIDAURRI AND QUINTERO

By 1861 the problem of how to maintain his autonomy seriously troubled Vidaurri. As far as the *norteños* were concerned, he had given them a sound, progressive government. The vigorous leadership he had provided resulted in economic and political stability. Mexicans in all regions hoped for such a strongman as Vidaurri, who would remain a popular and powerful governor as long as he could serve the primary needs of his subjects. But once he failed to provide prosperity and security, his position was in danger, whether the threat was internal or foreign.[1]

President Juárez proved to be Vidaurri's greatest threat. Although Juárez, in control of Mexico City since January, 1861, still faced a grave financial crisis, he was unquestionably the strongest man in the capital and soon would begin to consolidate his control, probably at the expense of strong state governors such as Vidaurri.[2] Vidaurri must have considered several desperate measures in an effort to preserve his power before the American Civil War supplied him with an alternative.

One of the most pressing issues facing the newly established Confederacy in 1861 was recognition of its belligerency by the various world powers. There was little doubt in the South that recognition would come promptly, because the aggressive commercial politics and Manifest Destiny of the North had caused many Europeans to sympathize with the South. If this interest

[1] Raymond Vernon, *The Dilemma of Mexico's Development: The Roles of the Private and Public Sectors*, 30–31.
[2] Prieto to the state governors, in *Archivo Mexicano. Colección de leyes, decretos, circulares y otros documentos*, V, 208–220; Scholes, *Mexican Politics*, 62; Ralph Roeder, *Juárez and His Mexico*, I, 320–356.

were not enough, then certainly "King Cotton" would insure recognition. Prominent Confederates believed that cotton would be the tool which would eventually force the world to acknowledge the existence of the new nation.[3]

Because the textile industry was basic to the industrial revolution in both Britain and France, many agreed with Major W. H. Chase, a leading proponent of the King Cotton theory, that cotton would do all the Southerners insisted it would.[4] Even English economists were convinced of it. When England and France did not recognize the South immediately, the Confederates instituted their master plan. Not waiting for the strangling Union blockade to take effect, they agreed among themselves that no cotton would leave any Southern port. They believed that this embargo on the supply of cotton would cause the huge textile mills of Europe to close, putting thousands of men out of work. When the strain of unemployment became too great, the men would force their governments to break the blockade to get more cotton, thus insuring Southern independence.[5]

This majestic design failed to function properly from the very beginning. Britain had a large surplus of cotton when the Civil War erupted, and the Englishmen knew that there were tons of cotton on the docks of the principal ports of the South. They felt that when the economic necessities of the war fully exerted themselves, the Confederates themselves would be forced to "run" the blockade.

Momentarily foiled, but still believing in the certainty of their plans, the Southerners resorted to more desperate measures.[6] If no cotton existed in the warehouses and the Europeans knew that future supplies depended only on the success of the next year's crop, perhaps they would be stirred from their lethargy. Beginning

[3] Henry Blumenthal, "Confederate Diplomacy: Popular Notions and International Realities," *Journal of Southern History*, XXXII (May, 1966), 152–154.

[4] Frank Lawrence Owsley, *King Cotton Diplomacy: Foreign Relations of the Confederate States of America*, 12–13.

[5] James M. Callahan, *The Diplomatic History of the Southern Confederation*, 102, 159.

[6] Blumenthal, "Confederate Diplomacy," 154–171.

in 1862, the Confederates first curtailed production, then burned thousands of bales of cotton. "The time . . . has come to test the earnestness of all classes," wrote General G. T. Beauregard, "and I call on Patriotic Planters owning cotton in positive reach of the enemy to APPLY THE TORCH TO IT WITHOUT DELAY OR HESITATION."[7] The Southerners feared that if the Union captured any cotton it would be shipped immediately to Europe. Although this too failed to stimulate foreign intervention, the destroying of the valuable crop demonstrated the hope that the Confederates had placed in King Cotton. In fact, cotton was the very foundation of the Southern diplomacy from its inception.[8]

Neither a significant cotton producer nor a cotton buyer, Mexico, particularly Vidaurri's domain, nevertheless figured prominently in the reign of the King.[9] In case of a Union blockade–and most Southerners agreed that it was a certainty–Mexico would be the only neutral country which would not be cut off from the South, giving the producers an alternative to running the blockade, which was dangerous and unsure at best. But Mexico was even more important in the over-all scheme of Confederate diplomacy because it might be the instrument by which the South would gain its independence. President Jefferson Davis expected that some European power, probably France, would intervene in Mexico after the Civil War started.[10] He was just as certain that the United States would answer the challenge, and that war between the two powers would follow. The European power, then, would surely recognize

[7] *Texas Republican* (Marshall), May 10, 1862.
[8] Owsley, *King Cotton Diplomacy*, I, 43–50.
[9] J. Fred Rippy, *The United States and Mexico*, 234; Frédéric Mauro, "L'economie du nord-est et la résistance à l'empire," in Arturo Arnaiz y Freg and Claude Bataillon (eds.), *La intervención francesa y el imperio de Maximiliano*, 61–63.
[10] Davis was correct in assuming European intervention, but perhaps not for the right reason. For years European statesmen had been looking for an opportunity to intervene in the New World to establish a counterbalance against the United States. Napoleon III of France felt that the best that could come from a split in the Union was an opportunity to establish this stronghold in Mexico while the armies of America were otherwise occupied. Kathryn Abbey Hanna, "The Roles of the South in the French Intervention in Mexico," *Journal of Southern History*, XX (February, 1954), 5–7.

the independence of and seek alliance with the South.[11] Mexico was thus in many ways the "most vital foreign problem" that the Confederacy faced.[12]

President Davis commissioned John T. Pickett to represent the Confederacy before the Juárez regime. Pickett, a former United States consul in Veracruz, was apparently well qualified for the position. With instructions to establish friendly relations with the government, he proceeded immediately to Mexico City. Ideally, the South would ease itself into the position of friendship formerly occupied by the United States. Immediate recognition need not be demanded, although this was one of the ultimate purposes of his mission. A more urgent task was to secure a guarantee that the Juárez administration would not allow the United States to invade the South through northern Mexico. Pickett also was to strive for an agreement regarding peace along the border.[13]

Initially, all the Confederate diplomatic efforts in Mexico were the handiwork of Pickett, a rabid Southerner of very undiplomatic demeanor. While endeavoring to win the confidence of the Mexican government, he revealed his utter contempt for the country and its people in his dispatches to the State Department. Since all his messages were being confiscated in Matamoros and forwarded to President Juárez, any chance for success was ruined. At the same time a very capable United States minister, Thomas Corwin, blocked all his overtures. Unaware that Corwin was negotiating a loan of $11,000,000 to the Juárez government, Pickett confidently predicted that $1,000,000 "judiciously applied" would purchase Mexican recognition. Nor did he know that while Mexican Foreign Minister Manuel Zamacona promised him that no Union troops would be permitted to pass over Mexican soil, the Mexican Congress unanimously approved a resolution allowing American troops to march through Sonora on their way from California to Arizona.

[11] Burton J. Hendrick, *Statesmen of the Lost Cause: Jefferson Davis and His Cabinet,* 109–116.

[12] Confederate Secretary of State Robert Toombs to Quintero, Montgomery, May 22, 1861, in *Official Records of the Union and Confederate Navies in the War of the Rebellion,* Series II, Vol. III, 217. Quote is from Owsley, *King Cotton Diplomacy,* 87.

[13] Owsley, *King Cotton Diplomacy,* 89–90.

Government officials later tried to excuse themselves by explaining that they did not realize that the Confederacy claimed Arizona when the resolution was passed, but it was obvious that Pickett's efforts had failed completely.[14]

The Southerner aggravated an already bad situation by openly insulting liberal government officials and befriending supporters of Miguel Miramón's outcast conservative faction. By fighting with a Unionist sympathizer, he succeeded in jeopardizing his diplomatic amnesty. Following an unusual display of "fistic skill," he was arrested and suffered in jail for thirty days. Finally, after bribing the judge and other officials, he was freed and quickly returned to the South.[15]

Unaware of Pickett's earlier failures in the capital, the Confederate government sought to insure tranquility along the border through another approach. The officials realized that Mexico might evolve into their most important supply source and outlet to the world markets if the Union effectively blockaded Southern ports, thereby making northern Mexico a crucial area. Consequently, the State Department sent José Agustín Quintero to Monterrey to establish friendly relations with Vidaurri and to assure him of the Confederacy's friendliness.[16]

The Confederate State Department could hardly have chosen a better qualified man to send to Monterrey. Quintero, in fact, was the most effective and important of the many agents sent to Mexico.[17] The native Cuban but devoted Southerner had a varied and outstanding background. Born in Havana, Cuba, in 1829, Quintero reportedly entered Harvard College at the early age of twelve. He continued his studies, even after his father died, by

[14] Ibid., 90–97. For an excellent description of Pickett's diplomacy from a Mexican viewpoint, see José Fuentes Mares, *Juárez y la intervención*, 94–107. Quote is from Owsley, 91.

[15] Owsley, *King Cotton Diplomacy*, 93, 97–98, 100–102; Edward H. Moseley (ed.), "Documents—A Witness for the Prosecution: The Pickett Incident," *The Register of the Kentucky Historical Society*, LXVIII (April, 1970), 171–179. Quote is from Owsley, 97.

[16] Quintero to Confederate Assistant Secretary of State William M. Browne, Galveston, June 1, 1861, in John T. Pickett Papers.

[17] Owsley, *King Cotton Diplomacy*, 114.

teaching Spanish to support himself. While at Cambridge, he was supposedly an "intimate" of Henry Wadsworth Longfellow and Ralph Waldo Emerson. Returning to Cuba, Quintero finished a law degree, then went into journalism. He edited two influential newspapers: *El Ranchero,* a democratic, Spanish-language paper in San Antonio, and a Spanish-language illustrated paper published by the well-known New Yorker, Frank Leslie. Quintero was no newcomer to war. Prior to his alliance with the South he had fought for the cause of Cuban independence. After the Civil War started, he acted against the advice of his northern friends and enlisted in the Confederate army in Texas. He went with his company to Virginia, where he was eventually assigned to the diplomatic corps.[18]

Reaching Monterrey in June, 1861, Quintero addressed a letter to Governor Vidaurri assuring him of the peaceful and friendly intentions of the Confederacy. He also presented his credentials: letters of introduction from Confederate Secretary of State Robert Toombs and Texas Governor Edward Clark, documents which Vidaurri deemed important enough to publish in the *Boletín Oficial,* thereby destroying any secrecy which might have shrouded the mission.[19] But Quintero could hardly have arrived at a more advantageous time. Vidaurri had begun to worry about his security because of a centralization of authority under Juárez; he was further concerned about a possible foreign intervention because of Mexico's indebtedness.

Although Quintero's mission was supposed to have been secret

[18] After the war ended, Quintero worked for the Galveston *News,* then moved to New Orleans and practiced law. He wrote for the *Daily Picayune* (New Orleans) and served as New Orleans consul for Belgium and Costa Rica. He was an editor of the *Picayune* at the time of his death in 1885. See the *Daily Picayune,* September 8, 1885, p. 4; *Times–Picayune* (New Orleans), January 25, 1937, section A, p. 17. Although most biographical information on Quintero indicates that he was a student at Harvard, no record of his enrollment can be found in the Archives of Harvard College, Cambridge, Massachusetts. For other biographical material, see Gerardo Castellanos García, *Panorama histórico; esayo de cronología cubana, desde 1492 hasta 1933,* 352; *Cuba en la mano; enciclopedia popular ilustrada,* 989; Juan J. Remos y Rubio, *Resumen de historia de la literatura cubana,* 270–276.

[19] *Boletín Oficial* (Monterrey), July 3, 1861.

and confidential, obviously at no time during his tour of Mexico were the Union officials unaware of who or where he was. Soon after his first interview with Governor Vidaurri in June, documents appeared in the official paper over his name, clearly indicating that he was a Confederate agent. His subsequent return to Richmond and his reappointment to Monterrey did nothing to conceal his identity as a Southern agent, although they might have. There was no mention of his name in the Nuevo León paper upon his return, but this time his own countryman betrayed him. Soon after he arrived in Monterrey he was forced to visit Matamoros and Brownsville in an an attempt to settle a dispute between the filibustering forces of Carvajal and Vidaurri. In April, 1862, the editor of the *Fort Brown Flag* expressed utmost confidence that "Commissioner Quintero" would handle the situation ably. Again, in May, 1865, the editor of the *Daily Ranchero* praised the diplomat for his extraordinary work. Even the Union refugees from Texas knew of Quintero. If from no other source than newspaper coverage, then, Union Consul M. M. Kimmey knew about the "Confederate agent" in Monterrey.[20]

Discussions were facilitated because of the personal manner in which Vidaurri conducted governmental affairs, and because Quintero and the governor already were friends, having met in Austin during Vidaurri's brief exile in Texas in 1859. They had maintained a sporadic but cordial correspondence since that time and evidently greatly respected each other.[21]

---

[20] Ibid.; *Fort Brown Flag* (Brownsville), April 17, 1862; *Daily Ranchero* (Matamoros), May 24, 1865; U.S. Consul C. B. H. Blood to Secretary of State William H. Seward, Washington, August 17, 1862; Kimmey to Seward, Monterrey, October 29, 1862, in Monterrey Consular Despatches; Thomas North, *Five Years in Texas: or, What You Did Not Hear During the War From January 1861 to January 1866. A Narrative of His Travels, Experiences, and Observations, in Texas and Mexico*, 180; *State Gazette* (Austin), June 22, 1861. The *Texas State Gazette* went by numerous titles during the 1850's and 1860's, but all that are cited in this work are available on the same microfilm series which was made from the collection in the University of Texas Newspaper Collection. The copy used for this research is in the Newspaper Collection, Amon Carter Museum of Western Art, Fort Worth.

[21] Quintero to Vidaurri, Austin, June 2, October 27, 1860, in Correspondencia de Vidaurri.

47

Because he had to be very careful to represent the over-all goals of his government's diplomacy, Quintero probably felt slightly hampered. Mexico was of the utmost importance; therefore he adhered strictly to instructions. Vidaurri, on the other hand, had a great deal of latitude. He hoped to secure his realm in the negotiations with the South. He would discuss almost any matter in the hope of gaining support from the Confederacy, strength he could then use to negotiate with Juárez.

Through the intercession of Vidaurri's personal physician, Dr. J. H. Means, a former resident of South Carolina who was then a citizen of Monterrey, Quintero saw Vidaurri on June 23, 1861. Three days later, on June 26, Quintero was again able to undertake "confidential intercourse" with the governor. Quintero explained immediately that he was on a special mission which would last for only a few days. No considerations exceeded cordial relations with Vidaurri, he continued, and some agreement regarding the defense of the Rio Grande frontier was highly desirable. Since reliable information indicated that a large force was organizing in Mexico, Quintero expressed the hope that he could obtain Vidaurri's assistance in seeing that it never invaded Texas.[22]

The force to which Quintero referred had troubled Texans in previous years. Juan N. "Cheno" Cortina first rose to prominence in 1859 when his band of Mexicans captured and held Brownsville until a company of Texas Rangers expelled them. Because of the support of the Mexican peasants, he had reached the status of a folk hero and could raise a large force almost at will.[23] In 1861 Texans strongly suspected because of his organizing activities that he would again disturb the quiet of the border. At his instigation, some Mexicans residing in Texas reportedly had already pronounced against the government in Richmond, and the Confederate authorities expected more depredations from his force in Mexico.[24]

[22] Quintero to Vidaurri, Monterrey, June 19, 1861, and Toombs to Vidaurri, Montgomery, May 22, 1861, in Boletín Oficial (Monterrey), July 5, 1861. English translations may be found in the Pickett Papers.

[23] John S. Ford, Rip Ford's Texas, ed. by Stephen B. Oates, 262–266.

[24] Ibid., 324.

In addition to agreement concerning the defense of the frontier, Quintero's instructions from Secretary of State Toombs suggested further goals as well. The Confederate authorities were worried about the possibility of a Union invasion through northern Mexico. For months there had been rumors to that effect, and some serious efforts had been made by Union men, particularly in the western part of the United States, to obtain permission to march troops into the Confederacy through Mexico. In 1861 an invasion through Sonora was the most attractive proposition. Even if Juárez gave permission for such a march, Quintero might be able to prevent it by his efforts in the north.[25] He had orders from Secretary Toombs to extract a promise from Vidaurri that neither Mexican nor Union troops would be permitted to invade Texas through Nuevo León y Coahuila. Then he was to seek Vidaurri's aid in convincing the governors of the other northern states that their best interests would be served by making similar guarantees.[26]

Quintero also wished to explore with Governor Vidaurri the possibility of making a reciprocal extradition agreement which would enable the governments to reduce the number of criminals who crossed the Rio Grande to prevent capture. Armed parties had raided both sides of the river, and Secretary Toombs wanted Quintero to be firm but friendly as he explained to Vidaurri that the South was justified in complaining. At the same time, Quintero was to assure the *caudillo* that the Confederacy would initiate measures to prevent filibusters from entering his domain.[27]

If the interviews proceeded well, Quintero might suggest other points for discussion. The South would need a source of war materials, particularly arms, but also minerals such as lead and salt-

[25] See Fuentes Mares, *Juárez y la intervención*, 108–114, for a description of some of the Confederate activities in Nuevo León and Chihuahua. See also Rippy, *United States and Mexico*, 236–238.

[26] Toombs to Quintero, Montgomery, May 22, 1861, in *Official Records of the Navies*, Series II, Vol. III, 217. See also José Fuentes Mares, *Y México se refugió en el desierto; Luis Terrazas: historia y destino*, 47–71, for information on the relationship between Vidaurri and Governor Luis Terrazas of Chihuahua and on the Confederacy.

[27] Toombs to Quintero, Montgomery, May 22, 1861, in *Official Records of the Navies*, Series II, Vol. III, 217; Toombs to Vidaurri, Montgomery, May 22, 1861, in *Boletín Oficial* (Monterrey), July 5, 1861.

peter if the blockade of Southern ports were immediately effective. Mexico, of course, had been famous for rich deposits of natural resources for centuries. Therefore, Quintero was to inquire concerning the possibility of the South's trading for both domestic and
war supplies.[28]

Realizing that friendship with the South would bring the commerce that the north so badly needed and cement the informal
ties that had existed between that region and Texas for years,
Vidaurri responded more favorably than any Southerner could have
expected in the interviews on June 23 and 26. After noting that he
did not have the authority to conduct diplomatic relations with any
foreign country, the governor informed Quintero that because of
the extraordinary circumstances in this situation, he would act on
behalf of the national government. Not only did Vidaurri express
"great friendship" for the Confederacy, but he added that he was
determined to preserve border peace.[29] He further assured Quintero that Mexicans also considered Cortina an "irresponsible man"
and that he was being pursued, but regrettably, he had not yet
been captured.[30]

Vidaurri mentioned a request that he had made to Texas Governor Hardin R. Runnels in 1859 concerning the suppression of
crime, which eventually had been forwarded to the government in
Washington. In addition, he had issued a decree in April, 1861,
calling for the arrest and punishment of anyone crossing into Texas
for criminal purposes and returning to Mexico for safety. He pointed out to Quintero that this had been done without an official
extradition treaty between the two nations or any favorable response from Texas officials. Vidaurri continued, seemingly anticipating every issue that Quintero hoped to discuss, answering each
question satisfactorily for the South.[31] At the end of the series of
interviews, Quintero was elated.

[28] Quintero to R. M. T. Hunter, Richmond, August 16, 1861, in Pickett
Papers.
[29] Quintero to Browne, Brownsville, July 14, 1861, in Pickett Papers.
[30] Vidaurri to the Confederate State Department, Monterrey, July 1, 1861,
copy in Governors' Letters.
[31] Ibid.; Quintero to Hunter, Richmond, August 16, 1861, in Pickett Papers.

But there was still another expression of friendship by Vidaurri. The governor visited Quintero in his hotel room the evening before the diplomat was to depart for Texas. During an hour-long visit, Vidaurri again referred to "his friendship and good will" toward the Confederacy and requested that the visit be regarded as a "call on his Excellency Jefferson Davis."[32]

Obviously, Quintero's visit in Monterrey had been a complete success. In his dispatch assuring Southern Assistant Secretary of State William M. Browne that Union President Abraham Lincoln would never obtain Vidaurri's permission to send troops through his territory, Quintero proudly concluded, "We have gained an ally." To Governor Clark of Texas he wrote, "I have been entirely successful in my mission."[34]

Northern Mexico would be the South's only outlet through the Union blockade, but it was not a one-sided proposition. Vidaurri, of course, realized that he could use his new contact to great advantage. The northern Mexican states would be able to profit by high tariffs levied on the goods from Texas and by selling material to the Confederacy at exorbitant prices. But perhaps Vidaurri himself was most taken with the unfolding political opportunities. By allying himself with the strong Confederacy, he might be able to oppose successfully the centralist forces of Juárez and solidify his position in the north once again.[35]

Wisely protecting himself in case something should go wrong, Vidaurri informed Juárez that a representative of the Confederate government had called upon him in a very proper manner and was concerned about mutual problems.[36] To Foreign Minister Zamacona he wrote that Quintero had raised some very critical questions—particularly those of peace and security on the frontier—and he intended to give satisfactory answers.[37] He included in

[32] Quintero to Hunter, Richmond, August 19, 1861, in Pickett Papers.

[33] Quintero to Hunter, Richmond, August 16, 1861, in Pickett Papers.

[34] Quintero to Clark, Brownsville, July 11, 1861, in Governors' Letters.

[35] Owsley, King Cotton Diplomacy, 113.

[36] Vidaurri to Juárez, Monterrey, July 4, 1861, in Roel, Correspondencia, 73–74.

[37] Vidaurri to the Ministro de Relaciones Exteriores, Monterrey, July 3, 1861, in Jorge L. Tamayo (ed.), Benito Juárez: documentos, discursos y correspondencia, IV, 621–622.

the dispatch a copy of the *Boletín* that contained the correspondence with the Confederates. There was no secrecy about Quintero's original contact with Vidaurri.

A relieved Quintero meanwhile arrived at the newly established Confederate capital in Richmond, Virginia. The trip was a necessity; the agent felt that certain parts of his report could not be securely communicated by long distance mails because there were too many opportunities for interception by Union spies in the post office department. On August 17 Quintero began divulging the full content of his interviews with Vidaurri in a series of letters to the newly appointed secretary of state, R. M. T. Hunter.

It was well known to everyone on the border, Vidaurri had begun, that for several years he had been "anxious to establish the Republic of Sierra Madre," composed of the northern states of Mexico. With the advent of the American Civil War, however, outright annexation of these states by the Confederacy might be a better solution.[38] Vidaurri mentioned several reasons for his opinions. He had admired Americans for several years and felt that northern Mexico more nearly resembled the southern part of the United States, both geographically and psychologically, than it did southern Mexico, with its tropical climate and illiterate Indians. "God had made everything beautiful in Mexico, except man," Vidaurri concluded, indicating his disillusionment with Juárez and the liberals. Fortunately, there were "intelligent people" in northern Mexico who realized that numerous advantages could be had by association with the Confederacy. The Mexican states had huge amounts of mineral wealth that could be successfully mined—with adequate technical skill and an industrious labor force available from the South. Agriculture had not been developed in Mexico as it had been in the Confederacy. Mexico raised some cotton and had mills that could be vastly improved with Southern help. In addition, property would be safer after alliance with the South because of stricter law enforcement. Vidaurri insisted that these states would continue the process of Americanization already germinating in

[38] Quintero to Hunter, Richmond, August 17, 19, 1861, in Pickett Papers. See also Lilia Díaz (ed.), *Versión francesca de México. Informes diplomáticos* [1862–1864], III, 178. Quote is from August 19 dispatch.

the area, leading eventually to governmental stability which the progressive citizens so badly wanted.[39] Proponents of Manifest Destiny could not have asked for a more willing subject.

Vidaurri had convinced Quintero that he was sincere in his proposal, explaining that he foresaw important occurrences within Mexico that would soon facilitate the annexation. He only sought some Confederate assurance that his plan was acceptable. There would be trouble with the Juárez government, of course, but limited support from Texas—perhaps the 1,000 men that had been offered previously—would insure success. The governor suggested that if President Davis would appoint someone he trusted to negotiate this proposal with Vidaurri, discussions could begin immediately. The new agent was to contact L. B. Cain of the New Orleans firm of K. Marks & Company, who would supply him with a letter of introduction to Dr. Means, who then would introduce him to Vidaurri.

Limited by his instructions in replying to Vidaurri's fantastic offer, Quintero had only said that he would faithfully report it to the proper officials and maintain strictest confidence. Although Vidaurri's offer was not remotely covered by his orders, he had considered it his duty to listen to the governor and let the State Department make its own decision.[40]

On a more mundane subject, but one that would mean more to the Confederacy in the coming years, Vidaurri had shown less enthusiasm. He could not allow the South to obtain arms in Nuevo León y Coahuila because of his own persistent disagreement with the federal government; he insisted that ten or eleven cannon and fewer than 10,000 rifles—all that he possessed—might be needed for local defense. If the Confederacy ever became so strong that northern Mexico could be annexed without jeopardizing its own position, perhaps such material could be obtained.[41] Of course, if the Confederacy were that powerful, the guns would hardly be necessary. As proof that he was not holding back at this point,

---

[39] Quintero to Hunter, Richmond, August 19, 1861, in Pickett Papers; Lempriere, *Notes in Mexico,* 133. Quotes are from Pickett Papers.
[40] Quintero to Hunter, Richmond, August 17, 1861, in Pickett Papers.
[41] Quintero to Hunter, Richmond, August 19, 1861, in Pickett Papers.

Vidaurri produced a complete list of all the Nuevo León "ordnance stores" and gave a copy to Quintero.[42]

Vidaurri did offer to sell unlimited quantities of other vital supplies. With a thirty- to forty-day notice, the South could obtain any quantity of powder at a reasonable price. Lead could be purchased in Monterrey at $10.50 per *carga* (300 pounds), or delivered to Roma, Texas, on the Rio Grande, for $12.875. It might be brought to Galveston for six to eight cents per pound more. A price of $15.50 would buy one *quintal* (100 pounds) of copper or bronze for making cannon. Some of the metals such as copper and lead might need refining because of the crude methods of the Mexicans, Quintero suggested to the State Department, but the "hard" lead might contain enough silver to make smelting profitable. Quintero hoped that the deposits of saltpeter near Piedras Negras could be acquired in large amounts at a moderate price.[43] In fact, he already had written Texas Governor Clark telling him how to order war supplies. Dr. Means, Vidaurri's physician, was willing to be a go-between, or Clark could address José Oliver, a merchant in Monterrey, or P. M. López of the Brownsville and Matamoros firm of Trevins & Company.[44]

Transportation presented a problem, but Quintero had proposed several solutions. For material shipped from Europe, the ports of Tamaulipas could be used. Although not the governor of that state, Vidaurri exercised a "moral influence" over its administrators to the extent that any agreement made with him probably would be as reliable as if made with Tamaulipas Governor Juan J. de la Garza.[45] If the Union prohibited ships carrying contraband to land at Bagdad (the port for Matamoros), Quintero speculated, the cost of the long overland haul might be prohibitive. But if neutral ships

[42] Quintero to Browne, Richmond, August 22, 1861, in Pickett Papers.

[43] Ibid.; Quintero to Hunter, Richmond, August 19, 1861, and Quintero to Browne, Richmond, August 22, 1861, in Pickett Papers; Quintero to Clark, Brownsville, July 11, 1861, in Governors' Letters.

[44] Quintero to Clark, Brownsville, July 11, 1861, in Governors' Letters. Trevins & Company should probably be Treviño & Company, however, source has Trevins.

[45] Arturo González, *Historia de Tamaulipas*, 82–84.

could deposit their goods at Matamoros, the government could expect "cheap and abundant transportation."[46]

Even before he talked with Vidaurri, Quintero, at the suggestion of General Hugh McLeod, had also investigated the possibility of building a railroad through northern Mexico. He prepared a report stating that if the rails connected with the Mexican port of Mazatlán, Sinaloa, the Confederates would have an outlet to the Pacific. In addition, Quintero wrote, "It would bind northern Mexico in a common interest with us." He suggested two possible routes: one through Durango and another through Chihuahua. The Durango route offered many opportunities. A natural pass that followed the Río del Nombre de Dios, near the city of Durango, would solve some engineering problems, and there were large deposits of lignite coal along the way. But Quintero concluded that the Chihuahua route would be better because passage through the mountains would be easier.[47]

Almost unlimited resources awaited exploitation in the Mazatlán area. A deep-water harbor could easily service ocean-going vessels. Perhaps just as important were the numerous minerals that could be found along the proposed track route and near the coast: iron, silver, lead, antimony, tin, gold, marble in eight or nine different varieties, alabaster, selenite, hydraulic lime, quartz crystal–all easily obtainable. Various fruits and well-timbered areas could provide many necessities for the Confederacy.[48]

Quintero knew that any proposal involving railroad construction would appeal to Vidaurri. The governor had often mentioned his desire for better transportation in northern Mexico; a line such as Quintero suggested would have helped him in at least two ways. The railroad would have enriched the northern states by developing their natural resources, and it would have drawn Vidaurri closer to the Confederacy. When Quintero showed the railroad report to the governor and asked his opinion, he therefore reacted favor-

[46] Quintero to Browne, Richmond, August 22, 1861, in Pickett Papers.
[47] Quintero to Hunter, Richmond, August 20, 1861, in Pickett Papers.
[48] Ibid.

ably. In fact, he wanted a Spanish translation of the document, which Quintero readily supplied.[49]

In a final report, dated August 22, Quintero further explained Governor Vidaurri's position. The *caudillo* had reiterated that the border situation precluded selling arms to the Confederacy. However, as long as he maintained his strength he exercised considerable influence over the neighboring state of Tamaulipas, which would render the main northern port of Matamoros at the service of the South.[50]

No doubt all of Quintero's dispatches received long and serious consideration from Confederate diplomatic officials. On September 3, Assistant Secretary of State Browne informed him that his work in Monterrey met with the "entire approval" of the department. The mission was considered so successful—and so important—that President Davis had appointed Quintero as permanent and confidential representative in Vidaurri's capital.[51]

Along with the commendation, Browne included full instructions for the new undertaking. Quintero was to return to Monterrey "with all convenient dispatch" and resume communication with Vidaurri. He was to assure the governor that President Davis fully reciprocated in the desires to maintain peace on the border and "friendship and goodwill" between the two areas. Davis did not look so favorably, however, upon Vidaurri's suggestion that the Confederacy annex northern Mexico. Certainly it was in the interest of both peoples that "intimate social and commercial relations" continue, but it would be "imprudent and impolitic" for the South to annex the territory. As if he were interested, however, Browne did order Quintero to gather data on the states: "accurate and minute information" regarding population, races, classes; topography, products, mineral resources; exports, imports manufactures —in other words, the "general condition of the people," socially, economically, and politically.[52] Another important task was to deter-

[49] Ibid.

[50] Quintero to Browne, Richmond, August 22, 1861, in Pickett Papers.

[51] Browne to Quintero, Richmond, September 3, 1861, in James D. Richardson (ed.), *A Compilation of the Messages and Papers of the Confederacy, Including the Diplomatic Correspondence, 1861–1865*, II, 77–80.

[52] Ibid.

mine whether the United States had obtained permission to march troops through northern Mexico. He was instructed to use Vidaurri's influence as much as possible to avert such an occurrence.[53]

Further, he was to cover the possibility of purchasing war material for the Confederate army. Browne indicated a special interest in small arms, lead, powder, and saltpeter, and instructed Quintero to contract for 500 tons of lead and for 200,000 pounds of powder, to be delivered to Roma, Texas. He was also to look for other articles needed by the army while searching for the best possible method of transporting those goods to Texas. To induce Vidaurri to reconsider providing arms to the Confederary, Browne pledged that if he would sell to the South half or a considerable portion of the weapons in his possession, it "would be regarded as a most signal and valuable proof of his friendship." If this could not be arranged, however, Quintero was to solicit Vidaurri's advice as to where to purchase arms, perhaps from some adjacent state.

Finally, because Quintero's mission was to be "secret and confidential," he was to tell only Governor Vidaurri and other necessary persons the nature of his task. He was instructed to remain in Monterrey until he received further instructions, receiving compensation of $200 per month and $250 to cover travel expenses to Monterrey.[54] In order to accept this post, Quintero had to refuse a position as private secretary to newly elected Governor Francis R. Lubbock of Texas, which might not have been so dangerous, but would not have provided as much service to the Confederacy.[55]

It may seem paradoxical that President Davis did not quickly agree to Vidaurri's offer to annex the Mexican border states. Although it could have been an attempt by Vidaurri to test the Confederacy's willingness to add new territory to its domain, the offer was probably a troubled man's desperate grasp for the best possible solution. Vidaurri despaired of an easy answer to his problem, particularly after Zuazua's death. He might well have reasoned that membership in the Confederacy would solve his primary problem—maintaining power. Indeed, one of the fundamental principles

[53] Ibid.
[54] Ibid.
[55] Quintero to Lubbock, Monterrey, November 9, 1861, in Governors' Letters.

around which the Southern states organized was a guarantee of states' rights and sovereignty. A strong Confederacy could have protected the governor from Juárez and his centralist allies. Annexation also would have allowed him to establish more American institutions in Nuevo León y Coahuila, something Vidaurri felt would also help his people.

But President Davis was much too intelligent to make such a mistake. And he was following a policy that probably would have developed even if the South had won its independence. Whether realistic or not, Davis did expect several European powers to intervene in Mexico; France would probably try to establish a puppet government there. In such a circumstance the United States surely would challenge the interventionist, possibly leading to a war in which the European powers would be forced to recognize the Southern Confederacy. But if the South annexed Mexican territory, such a conflict might never materialize, and the South itself would incur the wrath of the empire-building power as well as render the northern Mexican ports subject to the Union blockade. In any event, such an annexation certainly would have brought a war with Juárez. Another negative factor that Davis probably considered more than once was that he had enough independently minded governors in the Confederacy already. He did not need another one.[56]

Quintero hurriedly left Richmond on his new mission. When he reached New Orleans he was shocked to hear that Governor Vidaurri had been expelled from Nuevo León and was in exile in Texas. Unwilling to accept unreliable newspaper reports or third-hand accounts, he went directly to Vidaurri's confidant in New Orleans, L. B. Cain, who reported that he had received several letters from the governor recently. Much to Quintero's relief, Cain expressed serious doubts that the federal government could have dislodged Vidaurri for the *caudillo* had been too well prepared. Uncertain as to Vidaurri's fate, however, Quintero wrote the State Department that he would remain in New Orleans awaiting further instructions.[57]

[56] Owsley, *King Cotton Diplomacy*, 116–117.
[57] Quintero to Browne, New Orleans, September 9, 1861, in Pickett Papers.

Quintero realized that the situation in Mexico was so unstable that General Ignacio Zaragoza's 6,000 soldiers might well have driven Vidaurri from Monterrey as had been widely rumored. Vidaurri had occupied a strong position in the north and therefore hampered efforts to centralize the government; also, his continual friction with Juárez had increased because of the widespread reports that the *caudillo* desired annexation to the Confederacy. He further antagonized Juárez when he gave refuge to a fellow Mason, former President Ignacio Comonfort, who had been exiled from the country following his resignation in January, 1858.[58] Arriving in Laredo on July 20, Comonfort found refuge with one of Vidaurri's friends, Santos Benavides. There he received a letter from the governor giving him permission to enter Nuevo León. He quickly wrote Vidaurri that he would leave Laredo immediately and would arrive in Monterrey no later than July 25.[59] When Juárez read that Comonfort had been allowed to enter the country, he ordered Vidaurri to arrest him and return him to Mexico City.[60] Vidaurri, however, responded with a long list of reasons as to why the ex-President should remain free.[61] Probably the main reason, which he did not cite, was that he thought Comonfort would make a valuable aide, and he soon gave the ex-President command of the Nuevo León militia.[62]

Although a fight could easily have broken out had Juárez sent troops into Nuevo León to arrest Comonfort, Quintero soon learned that no conflict had occurred. The troubled diplomat had "very

[58] Scholes, *Mexican Politics*, 23–24; Rosaura Hernández Rodríguez (ed.), *Ignacio Comonfort, trayectoria política. Documentos,* 13; Federico Berrueto Ramón, *Ignacio Zaragoza,* 214–215; Ray F. Broussard, "Ignacio Comonfort: His Contributions to the Mexican Reform, 1855–1857," 235–236.

[59] Comonfort to Vidaurri, Laredo, July 21, 1861, and Santos Benavides to Vidaurri, Carrizo, Texas, July 11, 1861, in Correspondencia de Vidaurri; Rosaura Hernández Rodríguez, "Comonfort y la intervención francesca," *Historia Mexicana,* XIII (julio-septiembre, 1963), 60; Ray F. Broussard, "Vidaurri, Juárez and Comonfort's Return From Exile," *Hispanic American Historical Review,* XLIX (May, 1969), 268–280.

[60] Tamayo, *Juárez: documentos,* I, 317–318.

[61] Vidaurri to Juárez, Monterrey, July 4, August 9, September 29, 1861, in Roel, *Correspondencia,* 73–74, 77–82.

[62] Hernández Rodríguez, *Ignacio Comonfort,* 13; Broussard, "Comonfort," 238.

cautiously" approached the Mexican consul in New Orleans for the latest information, part of which 'was a letter from Comonfort himself.[63] Browne immediately telegraphed Quintero to proceed to Monterrey and begin his confidential mission. Leaving in mid-September, Quintero went through Brownsville where he conferred with Confederate authorities, then on to Monterrey where he arrived in late October. By early November he had established himself in Vidaurri's capital and soon began sending back some of the more important dispatches of the war.[64]

[63] Quintero to Browne, New Orleans, September 18, 1861, in Pickett Papers. Perhaps one reason Quintero was able to get information from the Mexican consul and Comonfort had written that official was that Comonfort had firm friends among the Masons in New Orleans. See letter from New Orleans Lodge Number 9 to "ALL MASONS DISPERSED OVER THE TWO HEMI-SPHERES," March 27, 1859, in Hernández Rodríguez, *Ignacio Comonfort,* 160–162.

[64] Quintero to Hunter, Brownsville, October 18, Monterrey, November 4, 1861, in Pickett Papers.

CHAPTER III

THE ONLY CHANNEL

Like many regional *caudillos,* Vidaurri held influence beyond his state boundaries–even though, in this instance, his domain encompassed what formerly had been two separate states. From the moment of his takeover in 1855, he was a respected power in Coahuila, Tamaulipas, San Luis Potosí, Chihuahua, and Durango. By 1862 he had legal authority in Tamaulipas, giving him more control over the northern frontier of Mexico than any man had exercised for decades. He was therefore even more valuable to the Confederates. And he drew closer to his personal goal of domination of all the north.

Tamaulipas was not governed by one figure as was Nuevo León y Coahuila. Jesús de la Serna, known to be a Confederate sympathizer, had been elected governor of the state in the fall of 1861. After a careful scrutiny of the votes, the national government, under President Juárez, declared him the legally elected governor, but some were dissatisfied with the results. Cipriano Guerrero, the opposing candidate, gathered his friends and pronounced against Serna. Serna, of course, defended his governorship, and northern Mexico was soon in the midst of another revolution.[1]

Serna turned to General José María Jesús Carvajal, the well-known filibuster, and his band of *rojos.* The general commanded the attention and respect of most Americans on the border. Educated at Bethany College in Virginia, Carvajal was described by the editor of the *Fort Brown Flag* as "a very intelligent gentleman" who spoke "English 'like a book.'" The newsman visited the gener-

[1] Quintero to Hunter, Brownsville, October 18, 1861, in Pickett Papers; *Tri-Weekly Civilian* (Galveston), November 12, 1861; González, *Historia de Tamaulipas,* 81–82; Díaz, *Versión francesa,* III, 86–97.

al in his camp and interviewed him. During their talk Carvajal referred to the "intimacy" between himself and the Confederates and mentioned that his two sons were then protecting a "Southern school" from a Northern invasion, an obvious effort to gain the sympathy of those in Brownsville who might help him in his battle against Guerrero and his forces.[2]

Guerrero, meanwhile, had chosen an equally able commander, General Guadalupe García, to direct his *crinolinos,* or *amarillos,* as his followers were known, in their effort to overthrow Serna. The editor of the *Fort Brown Flag* also visited García's camp and came away impressed. General García "speaks with confidence, and denies all possibility of . . . failure," reported the editor. He "is an agreeable gentleman and most popular officer" whose "presence is the strength of the garrison." García now commands from 800 to 1,200 soldiers "who manifest an earnest disposition to fight until the bitter end," concluded the Brownsville newspaper man.[3]

The approaching conflict portended nothing but trouble for the Confederacy. The businesses that had so quickly thrived in Matamoros ground to a halt. "The lately flourishing city now looks like a grave yard . . .," reported the editor. "It is dangerous to approach the town in any direction, for fear of the flying bullets . . . ."[4] The struggle also threatened to involve the Southerners when General García enlarged the dispute to international proportions. After extracting a forced loan from the merchants of Matamoros, he expelled to Texas those whom he suspected of favoring Serna. Once across the Rio Grande, the merchants began to lay plans to return and seek their revenge. Because neutrality seemed impossible, the upheaval appeared certain to destroy Confederate influence and success in northern Mexico. As soon as Quintero arrived in Brownsville, en route to Monterrey, he learned of the tense situation in Tamaulipas. He also saw that if Serna finally won, there would be a good chance that Southern domination of north-

[2] *Weekly Texas State Gazette* (Austin), December 21, 1861, quoting the *Fort Brown Flag* (Brownsville).
[3] Ibid.
[4] Ibid.

ern Mexico would increase. Still there were such particularly deli-
cate problems as neutrality involved in the struggle.

When it became obvious that Serna's supporters were organizing
an expedition to return to Tamaulipas, Confederate Colonel John
S. Ford, commander of the Southern troops at Brownsville who
had been with Carvajal during an 1851 excursion into Mexico, dispersed them and informed both parties that he intended to observe
a strict neutrality.[5]

But the situation became more serious. On November 15 Carvajal moved his troops within five miles of Matamoros and began
drilling and arming them and laying plans for the attack. The residents of the city threw up hastily built barricades around the main
plaza, and officials from both forces notified the foreign consuls
and foreign citizens that they should mark their property so it
would not be attacked or destroyed during the fighting. General
García, the *comandante* of Matamoros, defended the city, according to one estimate, with approximately 500 cavalrymen and hundreds of infantrymen. On the morning of November 20, Carvajal
commenced what the correspondent for the Brownsville *Flag* called
a "lively charge" that sounded to the citizens of Brownsville like
"three thousand muskets had all exploded at once." Advancing in
columns, the *rojos* "shouted with enthusiastic gusto, 'Viva Pena!'
'Viva Treviño!' 'Viva Carvajal!' " And from behind their barricades
the *amarillos* called back, " 'Viva Garcia!' 'Viva Capistran!' 'Death
to the Traitors!' " The carnage, which soon attracted the attention
of most Brownsville residents across the border, spurred the military
into action. The Confederates blocked the ferries across the Rio
Grande, allowing no one to cross until Carvajal requested that he

[5] Quintero to Hunter, Brownsville, October 18, in Pickett Papers; González,
Historia de Tamaulipas, 82. In 1851 Carvajal, in an effort to win independence
for a portion of northern Mexico and to get trade for south Texas, raided into
Mexico at Matamoros and several other points. John S. Ford and some discharged Texas Rangers were with him, hoping that they could aid in setting
up a republic in northern Mexico, which they hoped would serve as a buffer
state between slave territory (Texas) and free territory (Mexico). Ford and
Carvajal thus were friends from at least 1851. They also were Masonic brothers.
See Ernest Shearer, "The Carvajal Disturbances," *Southwestern Historical
Quarterly*, LV (October, 1951), 201–230; Tyler, "The Callahan Expedition of
1855," 574–585.

be allowed to bring his wounded to the Texas side of the river. "The assault is fiercely conducted and as fiercely resisted," concluded the correspondent for the *Flag*. Nothing was decided.[6]

By December, 1861, most of the trade between Matamoros and Monterrey had been cut off, forcing Vidaurri to demand a loan from the merchants, some of whom were Texas Germans living in Monterrey to escape the Civil War.[7] The South, too, was suffering inconveniences. Because of Caravajal's siege all communications to Matamoros were halted, and Quintero had to send his messages directly to Brownsville by express.[8] All sides could see that the Tamaulipas dispute contained the seeds of a dangerous conflict.[9]

After several months of ineffective skirmishing with neither faction gaining control of the state, President Juárez declared Tamaulipas under martial law and appointed Vidaurri commander of all its forces, with full administrative power. Probably the main reason for his appointment was the fact that the French, Spaniards, and English were preparing an invasion, and Juárez wanted to strengthen defenses along the northern coast.[10] But with this new opportunity to expand his influence legally, Vidaurri could serve several causes equally well. He had succeeded in acquiring more personal power. He could defend northern Mexico as well as any official. And he could also help the Confederacy, since he understood its principles and had already conducted long discussions with Quintero.

Vidaurri first raised an army to occupy the port cities of Tampico, Soto la Marina, and Matamoros.[11] But General Carvajal, who had besieged Matamoros for several months, was unwilling to step

[6] *Texas Republican* (Marshall), December 21, 1861, quoting the *Fort Brown Flag* (Brownsville).

[7] Quintero to Hunter, Monterrey, November 16, December 1, 2, 1861, in Pickett Papers; González, *Historia de Tamaulipas*, 82.

[8] Quintero to Lubbock, Monterrey, December 2, 1861, in Governors' Letters; *Boletín Oficial* (Monterrey), December 8, 1861.

[9] Quintero to Lubbock, Monterrey, November 28, 1861, in Governors' Letters.

[10] *Boletín Oficial* (Monterrey), January 14, 1862; Vidaurri to Juárez, Monterrey, January 14, 1862, in Roel, *Correspondencia*, 107.

[11] Quintero to Hunter, Monterrey, February 1, 1862, in Pickett Papers.

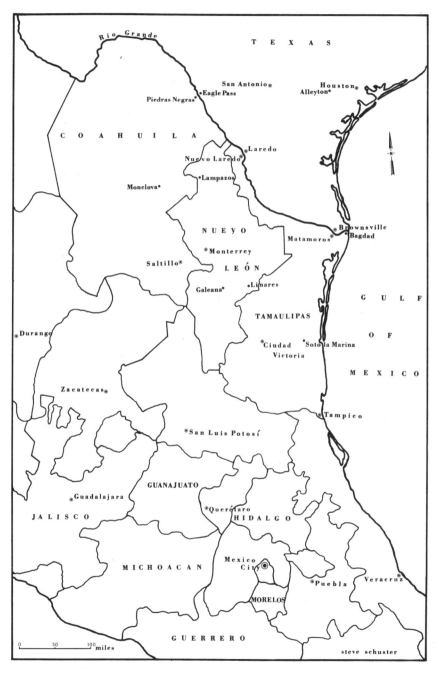

Map by Steve Schuster

out so quickly and easily.[12] Vidaurri then proposed that he and
Serna meet for discussions in Montemorelos, a village southeast of
Monterrey. Whether they actually met remains a mystery, but it
is certain that if a conference did indeed take place, there were no
discernible results.[13] Still, Governor Vidaurri was not caught off
guard. He had earlier ordered Colonel Julián Quiroga to proceed
to Matamoros with some 600 riflemen to guard the city against
further attacks by Carvajal.[14] Realizing that Carvajal was a friend
of many of the Confederates and probably would seek refuge in
Texas, Vidaurri asked Quintero to go to Brownsville to talk with
Colonel Philip N. Luckett, the commander of the Southern troops
there. By the time Quintero had reached the coast, both Serna
and Carvajal were in Brownsville, and they did not intend to give
up the fight.[15]

The Confederacy now faced a potentially serious problem: to
choose between a legally elected governor who reportedly favored
the South, and Vidaurri, who had already proven his extreme value
as an ally. Should the South support Serna, Vidaurri would block
all trading opportunities in Nuevo León y Coahuila. But if the
South supported Vidaurri and Serna won control of Tamaulipas,
Serna would close the port of Matamoros to the Confederates.
There was, however, no doubt in Quintero's mind as to which
course the South should follow. Vidaurri presented more opportunities and support. It also was likely that Vidaurri would win
the conflict.

If Quintero had not willingly come to that conclusion, Vidaurri
stood ready to pressure him—and for good reason. Because Colonel
Luckett apparently had attempted to maintain a strict neutrality,
the border seemed peaceful at first, but open fighting soon erupted
again. When the *rojos* first crossed into Texas, Luckett confiscated
their artillery and small arms; he also ordered two companies of

[12] *Boletín Oficial* (Monterrey), January 24, 26, 1862; Quintero to Hunter,
Monterrey, February 1, 1862, in Pickett Papers.
[13] Quintero to Hunter, Monterrey, February 1, 1862, in Pickett Papers;
Boletín Oficial (Monterrey), January 26, 1862.
[14] Quintero to Hunter, Monterrey, February 1, 1862, in Pickett Papers;
Boletín Oficial (Monterrey), January 24, February 19, 1862.
[15] Quintero to Browne, Brownsville, March 4, 1862, in Pickett Papers.

cavalry to patrol the Texas side of the river.[16] But he was replaced
in March, 1862, by Colonel Ford, who had returned from a brief
rest in San Antonio.[17] Quintero conferred with Ford, leaving no
doubt that as far as he was concerned the advantages lay in allying
with Vidaurri and that he expected Ford to keep Carvajal and
Serna from using Texas as a base of operations.[18]

With the reappointment of Ford, however, the question of
whether the South would remain strictly neutral seriously troubled
Vidaurri. The decision rested with Ford because his government
had remained silent. The governor felt that Ford would favor Carvajal, his long-time ally, thus diminishing Vidaurri's power in
Tamaulipas. Attempting to keep the colonel from aiding Carvajal,
Vidaurri penned notes to the Confederate State Department, President Davis, and Governor Lubbock reiterating his friendship and
willingness to furnish munitions for the Southern armies.[19] To add
emphasis to his appeals, he asked Quintero to deliver them personally to Richmond. Then, as military *comandante* of Tamaulipas,
Vidaurri claimed the arms and artillery taken from the *rojos* when
they crossed into Texas.[20]

Gradually Quintero ceased to trust Ford to guard the best interests of the Confederacy. He did report that Ford would probably
deliver the munitions in question to Colonel Quiroga, whose command had burgeoned to 2,000 men. But reasonably credible rumors
circulated that Carvajal was organizing troops in Texas and would
soon join Serna, who had returned to Mexico. This was despite the

[16] Ibid.; Quintero to Vidaurri, Brownsville, March 4, 1862, in Correspondencia de Vidaurri; *Fort Brown Flag* (Brownsville), April 17, 1862; Luckett
to Major E. F. Gray, Fort Brown, May 12, 1862, in *The War of the Rebellion:
A Compilation of the Official Records of the Union and Confederate Armies*,
Series I, Vol. LIII, 807–808.

[17] Ford, *Rip Ford's Texas*, 329, 332.

[18] Quintero to Browne, Brownsville, March 4, 1862, in Pickett Papers.

[19] Vidaurri to Jefferson Davis, Monterrey, January 25, 1862, in Correspondencia de Vidaurri; Vidaurri to Lubbock, Monterrey, March 10, 1862, in Governors' Letters.

[20] Quintero to Browne, Brownsville, March 8, Monterrey, March 22, 1862,
in Pickett Papers; Vidaurri to Quintero, Monterrey, March 10, 1862, in Correspondencia de Vidaurri; Vidaurri to Lubbock, Monterrey, March 10, 1862,
in Governors' Letters.

Benito Juárez, President of Mexico, 1858–1872.

Courtesy Library of Congress.

Ignacio Comonfort, President of Mexico, 1855–1858.

Courtesy Museo de Historia, Castillo de Chapúltepec.

fact that Ford assured Vidaurri that any such force would be broken up. Carvajal's activities probably caused Quiroga to be openly friendly with Leonard Pierce, Jr., the Union consul in Matamoros, earning himself a reputation as a "warm advocate" of the North.[21] Quintero expressed the fear that if the Texas authorities did not quickly and properly deal with Carvajal he would cause serious trouble. "It is not improbable," he continued, "that he will . . . make secret propositions" to the Confederacy through Colonel Ford.[22] His confidence in Ford diminished even more when Vidaurri claimed that the *rojos* were being allowed to publish their proclamations in Brownsville and purchase their cannon from Mifflin Kenedy and their ammunition from Treviño and Company, both owners of border firms. "I fear *he is not* mistaken," concluded Quintero. Apparently wasted were all the conferences in which Quintero had pleaded with Ford to maintain good terms with Vidaurri. Although Vidaurri was still willing to sell material to the South, Quintero reasoned that if Ford continually permitted Carvajal to organize troops in Texas, Governor Vidaurri would withdraw his offer and his friendship.[23]

The situation deteriorated rapidly. Leading an estimated 500 men, Carvajal crossed into Mexico in March, 1862, and attacked Reynosa.[24] There was strong evidence that he had received aid from someone in Texas, perhaps Ford, because he attacked with three cannon, the same number that had been taken from him earlier. Appealing to Governor Lubbock to refuse asylum to the raiders, Quintero pointed out that Vidaurri had 2,000 men in Matamoros, 1,000 in Tampico, and 3,000 under General Comonfort in Cuidad Victoria. Carvajal, he remonstrated, had little hope for success under such circumstances.[25] Quintero added that there was

[21] Pierce to Seward, Matamoros, March 24, 1862, in Despatches From United States Consuls in Matamoros, 1826–1906: Vols. VII–IX, January 1, 1858–December 28, 1869; *Fort Brown Flag* (Brownsville), April 17, 1862. Quote is from Matamoros Consular Despatches.

[22] Quintero to Browne, Monterrey, March 22, 1862, in Pickett Papers.

[23] Quintero to Browne, Monterrey, March 24, 1862, in Pickett Papers.

[24] Ibid.; *Fort Brown Flag* (Brownsville), April 17, 1862.

[25] Quintero to Lubbock, Monterrey, March 24, 1862, in Governors' Letters; *Boletín Oficial* (Monterrey), March 19, 1862.

a very good chance that this incident might seriously impair relations with Vidaurri.

Vidaurri, however, "acted with moderation and . . . friendliness." During an interview with Quintero he pointed out that Carvajal and Ford had been friends for years and that undoubtedly they were cooperating. Mentioning that Texans had been allowed to pursue Cortina into Mexico in 1859, Vidaurri requested permission from the Confederacy to chase Carvajal into Texas. Writing this in his report to the State Department, Quintero also warned that "*serious difficulties*" were near, that Quiroga and Ford had already exchanged "threatening communications," and that the "friendly relations with the Mexican frontier . . . [were] *fast dying away.*"[26]

Following his first letter to Governor Lubbock, Quintero authoritatively abstracted the situation in a confidential note. The attacks had not been limited to Reynosa, but also occurred at several other points along the border. Colonel Quiroga only just suspected that Carvajal had been allowed to prepare his force near Brownsville, under the fatherly protection of Ford, but Quintero knew that Kenedy and Treviño, who was also the Mexican consul in Brownsville, had furnished him with arms and ammunition. Several pleas that Colonel Ford disarm the filibuster had gone unheeded, causing Quintero to fear that Vidaurri would be forced to join Juárez in favoring the Union. Quintero concluded that without a change of course grave trouble faced the South.[27] Vidaurri eloquently appealed to Governor Lubbock for the revolutionists to be "disarmed and disbanded . . . and obliged . . . to live honestly."[28]

After no favorable results and several frustrating experiences, Quintero felt totally ineffective. He had repeatedly written to Ford on the issue. He had addressed dispatches to Governor Lubbock and Colonel McCulloch—he had done everything he could. Apparently that was insufficient. He concluded that there was only one

---

[26] Quintero to Browne, Monterrey, March 28, 1862, in Pickett Papers.

[27] Quintero to Lubbock, Monterrey, March 28, 1862, in Governors' Letters. Because of his complicity in the Carvajal affair, Treviño was recalled by the Mexican government, but he stayed in Brownsville, insisting that the order was illegal. *Fort Brown Flag* (Brownsville), April 17, 1862.

[28] Vidaurri to Lubbock, Monterrey, April 6, 1862, in Governors' Letters.

Juan Álvarez, President of Mexico, 1855.

Courtesy Museo de Historia, Castillo de Chapúltepec.

Juan Zuazua, Vidaurri's military chief, 1855–1859.

From Federico Berrueto Ramón, *Ignacio Zaragoza*.

thing left to do. To Assistant Secretary Browne he wrote, "I earnestly request the Department to appoint a person to succeed me who may have more influence . . . with the military at Brownsville."[29]

Quintero's dramatic threat to resign apparently had little immediate effect in Texas. The Mexican refugees once again crossed the Rio Grande and sacked the Nuevo León village of Guerrero. Indignant over the laxity of the Confederates, Vidaurri not only threatened to terminate all commerce with the South, but also to send troops into Texas to chastise the marauders as the Americans had done in Mexico in 1859.[30] Quintero, in fact, was informed that the border had been closed without any warning. On April 8, Colonel James N. Langstroth, a Confederate sympathizer from Monterrey, reported that he had asked Manuel G. Rejón, Vidaurri's secretary, for permission to cross at Mier, only to be told that Governor Vidaurri refused. The various disturbances, particularly the Carvajal raids, Langstroth said, had forced the closing.[31]

Vidaurri had retaliated, as Quintero had often predicted he would. Although the border was not closed for long, a duty of two cents per pound was placed on cotton and Matamoros ceased to be a free port. Vidaurri did not really want to hamper the trade. He only wanted to force the Confederates to give him more help in situations where they had the power to aid him. When Quintero asked for an explanation of the increase in duty, Vidaurri indicated that he would discuss the matter.[32] Later, in a private interview with Quintero, he claimed the duty on cotton was only a small part of an over-all effort to raise the thousands of dollars necessary to keep his army of 7,000 men in the field. He had already forced a loan from the merchants of Monterrey, he emphasized, which had proved insufficient.

[29] Quintero to Browne, Monterrey, March 28, 1862, in Pickett Papers.
[30] Quintero to Browne, Matamoros, April 17, 1862, in Pickett Papers; Quintero to Lubbock, Brownsville, April 13, 1862, in Governors' Letters; *Fort Brown Flag* (Brownsville), April 17, 1862.
[31] Quintero to Vidaurri, Brownsville, April 12, 1862, in Correspondencia de Vidaurri; Quintero to Lubbock, Brownsville, April 13, 1862, in Governors' Letters; Quintero to Browne, Matamoros, April 17, 1862, in Pickett Papers.
[32] Quintero to Vidaurri, Monterrey, April 4, 1862, in Pickett Papers.

Quite unimpressed by these arguments, Quintero contended that no duties would have been levied on cotton had the Texans been diligent in their role of preventing forays into Mexico. Although Vidaurri denied that this was the reason for the tariff, Quintero assured his superiors in the Confederate State Department that if they made sure there were no more attacks on Mexican villages by refugees in Texas, he could get a satisfactory solution for the economic problem.[33]

Quintero was soon vindicated. Evidence proving that he had fully understood the situation was forthcoming. On April 5, the day following their interview, Vidaurri lowered the new duty by 50 percent—from two cents per pound to one cent.[34] As a result of Quintero's requests, the Confederate government furthermore ordered Colonel Ford to arrest Carvajal if he persisted in fitting out expeditions on Texas soil.[35] The order obliged Ford to place duty above friendship. Quintero had long believed that although Ford was doing nothing to aid Carvajal, because of their longstanding friendship he was doing nothing to hinder him either. Meanwhile, Carvajal had established his camp within four miles of Brownsville and seemed determined to test the neutrality of the South. In an effort to prove to Vidaurri that Carvajal would be denied his sanctuary in Texas, Quintero notified Colonel Macedonio Capistrán, the new *comandante* in Matamoros, that he could initiate legal proceedings against the filibuster. He could charge him with violation of the international boundary in an affidavit sworn before Commissioner John Tabor in Brownsville. The Confederate army, then, would be forced to take action to prevent Carvajal from raiding into Tamaulipas or Nuevo León. The procedure was so successful that Quintero reported that the *rojo* party was soon disbanded and tensions between the Confederacy and Vidaurri were eased.[36]

[33] Quintero to Browne, Matamoros, April 17, 1862, in Pickett Papers.

[34] Vidaurri to Quintero, Monterrey, April 5, 1862, in Pickett Papers.

[35] Quintero to Browne, Matamoros, April 28, 1862, in Pickett Papers; McCulloch to Lubbock, San Antonio, April 16, 1862, in Governors' Letters; *Civilian Extra* (Galveston), May 8, 1862.

[36] Quintero to Browne, Matamoros, April 17, 28, 1862, and Quintero to Confederate Secretary of State Judah P. Benjamin, Matamoros, July 5, 1862, in Pickett Papers.

José Agustín Quintero y Woodville, Confederate agent in Monterrey, 1861–1865.

From José Manuel Carbonell, *Los poetas de "El Laud del Desterrado."*

José María Jesús Carvajal, wood engraving from a photograph, 1865.

From *Harper's Weekly*, January 13, 1866.

Vidaurri again had demonstrated how much he was willing to risk to sustain and expand his personal power. He had felt weak enough to propose that the Confederacy annex Nuevo León y Coahuila, but within less than a year he threatened to disrupt completely the relationship that he had established with the South in order to maintain his own realm. He was successful in this instance because Quintero strongly agreed with him, and because he negotiated from a position of strength—Vidaurri controlled the only neutral port open to the Confederacy, as well as a significant amount of trade.

A good relationship with Vidaurri was important to the Confederacy because the threat of a Union invasion through Mexico was still very real. Returning from a trip to Matamoros where he had heard such rumors, Quintero roused Vidaurri from his sick bed to inquire whether Northern troops had been given permission to pass through Mexican territory. Vidaurri replied that he had received no official communication on the subject, but that his friends in Mexico City had reported that indeed such permission had been granted; he added that 3,000 American soldiers would land at Guaymas, Sonora, and march into Arizona. Quintero requested that Vidaurri and one of the most influential members of the Nuevo León y Coahuila legislature write the Sonora governor to emphasize the need for maintaining peace along the border. They obliged. Quintero, however, soon learned that the threat of invasion was only a rumor. Instead, a postal treaty had been concluded between the North and the Juárez regime.[37]

Quintero was glad to be able to solicit Vidaurri's aid again in a similar matter. In March, 1862, he learned that although the Juárez administration had earlier refused permission, the United States was again trying to get approval from Governor Luis Terrazas of Chihuahua to pass troops through his state to Arizona Territory. A Confederate agent, Colonel James Reily, had gone to Chihuahua earlier and had come away believing that he had secured a promise that the frontier would be closed to the Union. Since Sonora and Chihuahua were much closer to Unionist Califor-

[37] Quintero to Hunter, Monterrey, November 4, 1861, February 1, 1862, in Pickett Papers.

nia, apparently those governors had acted more cautiously than Vidaurri or the Tamaulipas executives. Their diplomatic language probably confused Reily, for although he boasted that he achieved complete success, they had made few concessions.[38] After writing to General Edward H. Jordan in Chihuahua, Quintero learned that Governor Terrazas had given no such assurances. He also discovered that unfortunately Confederate Colonel John R. Baylor, thinking that invasion was imminent, had led between 200 and 300 troops into Chihuahua.[39] Quintero persuaded Vidaurri to have his secretary of state write the Juárez government, reminding the officials of their previous refusal to grant the United States permission to march across Mexican territory, and advising that such permission not be given.[40]

By July Vidaurri so favored the South that his friendship survived an increased diplomatic offensive by the North and a direct order from President Juárez. Thomas Corwin, the United States minister in Mexico City, had already concluded the postal treaty with the Mexican government and for months had been negotiating a loan for some $11,000,000. And Juárez had affixed his signature to the first extradition pact between the two governments the preceding May.[41] The newly appointed United States consul, C. B. H. Blood, also gave Vidaurri an opportunity to increase trade with the Union if he would only issue a statement indicating that American commercial goods would be respected. "My official position is only remunerative through the position afforded in trade," Blood reminded Vidaurri. "If I may be granted the favor of an official letter from you, it may be of much personal service to me with capitalists to show that no seizure will be lived upon, or extortions exercised upon the capital trusted to my care."[42]

[38] Martin Hardwick Hall, *Sibley's New Mexico Campaign*, 50–51; Martin Hardwick Hall, "Colonel James Reily's Diplomatic Missions to Chihuahua and Sonora," *New Mexico Historical Review*, XXXI (July, 1956), 232–242.

[39] Quintero to Browne, Brownsville, March 4, Matamoros, April 28, 1862, and Jordan to Quintero, Chihuahua, March 18, 1862, in Pickett Papers.

[40] Quintero to Browne, Brownsville, May 8, 1862, in Pickett Papers.

[41] James M. Callahan, *American Foreign Policy in Mexican Relations*, 282–286; Luis G. Zorrilla, *Historia de las relaciones entre México y los Estados Unidos de América, 1800–1958*, I, 416–422.

[42] Blood to Vidaurri, Monterrey, June 20, 1862, in Roel Papers.

Landing of General Bank's army at Brazos Island, November 2.   Wood engraving from *Frank Leslie's Illustrated Newspaper*, December 5, 1863.

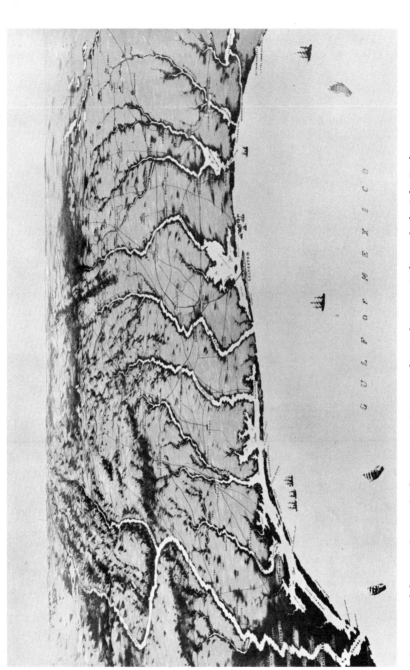

Panorama of the seat of war: a bird's eye view of Texas and part of Mexico. Lithography by John Bachmann.

Courtesy Amon Carter Museum, Fort Worth.

To Consul Blood's appeal for an official letter, Vidaurri replied that he could not comply with the request because of "public responsibility."[43] This response elicited an accusation from Blood that the "people of Texas were rebels and filibusters, far below the uncivilized Indians," but Vidaurri gave the statement only fleeting consideration and pledged to Quintero that he would continue supplying the Confederates whatever he could.[44]

Such leanings obviously disturbed Juárez. The President had written, on June 19, 1862, that Vidaurri should "cease all intercourse with the Confederate States, under whatever circumstances." Exportation of both commercial commodities and ammunition was forbidden. The new treaties and amicable relations with the Union, Juárez insisted, insured all the protection that Vidaurri might need. Vidaurri answered, however, that he was in an exceptional situation. The state of Neuvo León y Coahuila bordered Texas for hundreds of miles, and he had purposely cultivated good relations with the South. He would not destroy the cooperative atmosphere that he had encouraged, nor would he cut off trade because that would ruin the commerce of his state.[45]

Vidaurri and the Confederacy, therefore, maintained a working relationship, but border disturbances continually plagued them. On November 22, 1861, for example, a Confederate captain led approximately fifty volunteers into Coahuila near Piedras Negras. According to Vicente Garza, the commander of the Mexican forces on the frontier, the men were in search of a fugitive Negro slave. Although Garza insisted that no Negro had crossed the river, at least had not sought refuge in Piedras Negras, the Texans were not satisfied. Recalling the Callahan raid of 1855, the Confederates warned that if the Negro were not returned immediately, they would return with 150 men and burn the town. Attempting to discount the threat, Quintero had assured Vidaurri that the government would stop the expedition if it ever developed.[46] Then to insure that Vidaurri's realm remained protected from his aggres-

[43] Vidaurri to Blood, Monterrey, July 23, 1862, in Roel Papers.
[44] Quintero to Benjamin, Matamoros, July 5, 1862, in Pickett Papers.
[45] Ibid.
[46] Quintero to Hunter, Monterrey, December 1, 1861, in Pickett Papers.

sive countrymen, Quintero wrote to Governor Lubbock, Captain
H. A. Hammer, commander at Fort Clark, and Colonel Henry E.
McCulloch, the commander of the Western Department at San
Antonio, requesting that adequate steps be taken.[47] The problem
was soon solved. Quintero reported that Vidaurri was satisfied that
the foray had really been made at the request of several Mexican
citizens to chastise some Indians who troubled residents on both
sides of the border.[48]

Perhaps what infuriated patriotic Southerners most was the fact
that Vidaurri and other Mexican governors protected Union refugees fleeing from Texas and other parts of the South.[49] Thriving
colonies of Yankees resided in Monterrey, Matamoros, Piedras
Negras, and other border cities. The Union consuls in Matamoros
and Monterrey complained that they were surfeited by penniless
refugees and had no means to help them. After explaining that
his office was "constantly thronged with refugees from Texas,"
Consul Pierce requested that Secretary of State Seward "pass light-
ly over . . . [his] blunders."[50] Similarly overwhelmed by "destitute
Union men," then Vice-Consul Kimmey in Monterrey wrote that
"I am overrun with them" and "still without instructions."[51] He
had housed as many as thirty-two in his "rooms," but that only
amounted to just about 3 percent of those needing assistance. Over
1,000 of them were scattered along the frontier. In Piedras Negras
200 of these "renegades," as the Southerners called them, had great
difficulty in earning a living because they knew no Spanish. They
came until Monterrey was "full" and Matamoros looked like an
"American town." There were so many Americans in Matamoros
that they held Protestant services each Sunday morning in the
Varieties Theater in what Thomas North, himself one of the refu-

[47] Ibid.; McCulloch to Lubbock, San Antonio, February 19, 1862, in Governors' Letters; Quintero to Hammer, Monterrey, December 6, 1861, in
Boletín Oficial (Monterrey), December 22, 1861.

[48] McCulloch to Lubbock, San Antonio, February 19, 1862, in Governors'
Letters; *Boletín Oficial* (Monterrey), December 11, 1861.

[49] Quintero to Benjamin, Matamoros, August 30, 1862, in Pickett Papers.

[50] Pierce to Seward, Matamoros, March 16, 1862, in Matamoros Consular
Despatches.

[51] Kimmey to Seward, Monterrey, September 21, 1863, in Monterrey Consular Despatches.

Loading wagons on the Calle de Cesar, Matamoras, for Piedras Negras.

Frank Leslie's Illustrated Newspaper, February 20, 1864.

The Confederates evacuating Brownsville, Texas.

Wood engraving from *Harper's Weekly*, February 13, 1864.

gees, called a *"religio coup d'etat."*[52] Some left to join the Union army; others hoped to join any northern force invading through Texas. The remainder waited in Mexico until the war was over; then most returned to Texas.[53]

Some of the refugees were well-known residents of Texas that the Confederacy hated to see escape. E. J. Davis, formerly a district court judge and later Reconstruction governor of the state, and A. J. Hamilton, ex-congressman and later the provisional governor, were among the foremost. Nor were the Southerners content to see Hamilton and Davis residing just across the river in Matamoros, because they and other Unionists, such as William Montgomery, had openly recruited men to raid Texas and punish the Confederates for harboring Carvajal.[54] They stood just over the river, wrote the correspondent for the Tyler *Reporter,* and "began a series of indignities which were very provoking . . . their cowardly natures prompted them to peer at and insult our brave boys." On the evening of March 14, 1863, a group of Southerners, including the correspondent for the *Reporter,* crossed the Rio Grande and seized several Yankee refugees, most of them unidentified, but including Montgomery and Davis. "This we did at 4 o'clock a.m.," wrote the reporter. "Surrounding the house in which Col[onel] Davis was said to be, [we] . . . ordered [him] to surrender, and I regret to say, he did so." Successful, the Southerners returned to Brownsville, but "arrived safely with only one prisoner," Colonel Davis. The others had *"escaped,"* meaning that they had been murdered; officially they were said to have been shot while trying to escape. Montgomery was hanged from one of the wispy mesquite trees near Brownsville. Davis survived only because his

[52] Kimmey to Seward, Monterrey, November 21, 1862, April 7, 1863, in Monterrey Consular Despatches; Pierce to Seward, Matamoros, April 30, 1862, in Matamoros Consular Despatches; Jesse Sumpter, *Paso del Águila: A Chronicle of Frontier Days on the Texas Border,* ed. by Ben E. Pingenot, 93. Quotes are from North, *Five Years in Texas,* 172.

[53] Pierce to Seward, Matamoros, April 8, 1862, in Matamoros Consular Despatches.

[54] Quintero to Benjamin, Matamoros, August 30, 1862, Brownsville, January 20, Brownsville, February 26, Monterrey, March 21, 1863, in Pickett Papers; Owsley, *King Cotton Diplomacy,* 124.

wife, the daughter of a respected Confederate, was present when he was captured and successfully pleaded for his life.[55]

Quintero immediately reported to Vidaurri that the "bitter enemy of our cause" had been taken to Brownsville where he would be "permanently located."[56] But the governor did not appear overly concerned with Davis's capture, the only question in his mind being why it had not happened sooner. Vidaurri resented some of the citizens at Matamoros because they favored the Juárez government, which was beginning to pressure him. Therefore, he would not go out of his way to defend Matamoros, particularly if in doing so he would risk offending the Confederacy. Raids into Mexico would be made, he admitted, to avenge those recently made into Texas. Quintero, therefore, determined to wait until he heard officially from the Mexican government before he made any recommendation to the Confederate State Department. He realized, however, that the disturbance might well further complicate his mission.[57]

The violation of Mexican neutrality by the Confederates provoked an almost violent reaction in Tamaulipas. The day following the foray Matamoros was in a "blaze," and Governor Albino López demanded Davis's release. He threatened to discontinue all trading with Texas and arrest any Confederates found in Matamoros. Bands paraded through the streets playing patriotic music, and the people shouted *vivas* for the Lincoln government and death to the South. Because it appeared that he might take a lenient approach in the matter, Governor López was "hissed at" when he attended the theater. The people feared that the governor would not adequately press the demand that Mexican neutrality be observed.[58]

Although apparently without the support of the federal government, López's demands did win freedom for Davis and several others. The governor had threatened to close the border to all

[55] Tyler *Reporter*, April 16, 1863; Arthur James Lyon Fremantle, *The Fremantle Diary: Being the Journal of Lieutenant Colonel Arthur James Lyon Fremantle, Coldstream Guards, on His Three Months in the Southern States,* ed. by Walter Lord, 7–9.

[56] Quintero to Benjamin, Monterrey, March 21, 1863, in Pickett Papers.

[57] Ibid.

[58] Ibid.

Cotton press at Piedras Negras, on the Rio Grande.

Wood engraving from *Frank Leslie's Illustrated Newspaper*, September 3, 1864.

Matamoros, Mexico, opposite Brownsville.

Wood engraving from *Frank Leslie's Illustrated Newspaper*, December 5, 1863.

trade and arrest any Southerners in Matamoros. Clearly this was not worth the life of E. J. Davis, and Brigadier General Hamilton P. Bee, the new Confederate commander at Brownsville, returned the prisoners to the Mexican bank. But López had acted without authority, even though Juárez agreed with his position. He had received an order forbidding him to stop the foreign trade, but he neglected to publish it until after the incident. The minister of state announced that Mexico did not approve of the raiding parties organizing on its soil, but the government also did not approve of the Southerners' action and registered a diplomatic protest.[59]

Although they had hoped to catch ex-Congressman A. J. Hamilton in their dragnet (but did not), Confederate officials demonstrated a kinder attitude toward him than toward the other Unionists, perhaps because of a request made by Governor Vidaurri. On January 29, 1863, Vidaurri addressed both Quintero and Bee, informing them that Mrs. Hamilton, who lived in Austin, had written him requesting permission to join her husband in Mexico. Declaring that the decision was not his to make, although he saw no obstacles, Bee referred the matter to General John B. Magruder in Houston, who in turn sent it to the governor. Although he received a positive reply from the governor, Magruder contended that the "families of the . . . traitors . . . should be retained as hostages for the good conduct of our merciless enemies." But "in consideration of the liberal and friendly spirit" that Vidaurri had always demonstrated, he replied that Mrs. Hamilton could leave any time and cross the border at any place Vidaurri chose. After a delay of several months, Mrs. Hamilton was reunited with her husband.[60]

[59] Quintero to Benjamin, Monterrey, April 6, 20, 1863, in Pickett Papers.

[60] See extensive correspondence on this case: Quintero to Benjamin, Brownsville, February 26, 1863, in Pickett Papers; Vidaurri to Quintero, Monterrey, January 29, 1863, and Bee to Vidaurri, Fort Brown, February 9, 1863, in Correspondencia de Vidaurri; Vidaurri to Bee, Monterrey, January 29, October 23, November 12, 1863, Bee to Vidaurri, Fort Brown, October 27, 1863, Magruder to Vidaurri, Houston, October 11, 1863, Vidaurri to Magruder, Monterrey, October 23, 1863, and Vidaurri to Mrs. Hamilton, Monterrey, October 23, 1863, in Roel Papers.

Throughout the latter part of 1862 and early 1863 there was a real threat that the Unionists in Mexico would raid Texas, although Vidaurri continued to pledge neutrality. Certainly, if an American army landed the fugitives would join it. Quintero also feared that the Yankees might combine forces with Carvajal or some other Mexican who held a grudge against Texas.[61] There was a threat in Matamoros, another near Piedras Negras, and even the "miscreant" Kimmey, a fugitive from Texas himself, was rumored to be planning a raid.[62] Such reports and threats rapidly grew common. Octaviano Zapata, one of Cortina's lieutenants, armed parties near Guerrero, Mier, and other border points to invade Texas. Supposedly encouraged by Consul Pierce at Matamoros, they planned to rob and plunder the stock ranches across the border. Quintero, of course, protested to Governor López and was informed that steps had been taken to arrest the leaders of the movement, including Pierce if he were implicated.[63]

But the incursions came anyway. On December 18, 1862, a party of Mexicans crossed the river at Las Cuevas, attacked a Confederate wagon train, killed three teamsters, and returned to Mexico. Another group crossed near Rancho Clariño, just a few miles on the Texas side of the border, murdered the chief justice of Zapata County, Isidro Vela, then fled back into Mexico. These raiders did not go unpunished. Confederate Captain Santos Benavides, with a company of Mexican cavalrymen, crossed the Rio Grande near Camargo and attacked the robbers. He recounted that he had killed eighteen and wounded fourteen. Spoils amounted to fifty-eight horses, fifty-four saddles, and a cache of documents supposedly proving that Pierce had encouraged and supported the bandits.[64]

[61] Quintero to Benjamin, Monterrey, January 25, 1864, in Pickett Papers; Ford, *Rip Ford's Texas*, 351.

[62] Quintero to Benjamin, Matamoros, August 30, Monterrey, October 19, 1862, in Pickett Papers; Quintero to Vidaurri, Monterrey, November 23, 1863, in Correspondencia de Vidaurri.

[63] Quintero to Benjamin, Monterrey, December 1, 11, 1862, in Pickett Papers; *Boletín Oficial* (Monterrey), November 30, 1862; Vidaurri to the Minister of Foreign Relations, Monterrey, May 18, 1862, in U.S. Congress, *House Executive Documents*, 37th Cong., 3rd Sess., Document No. 54, pp. 19–20.

[64] Quintero to Benjamin, Brownsville, January 30, 1863, in Pickett Papers; Benavides to Vidaurri, Laredo, February 1, 1863, in Correspondencia de Vi-

Patricio Milmo, son-in-law of Vidaurri and leading Monterrey merchant.

Courtesy Sra. Berta Zambrano de Milmo, Monterrey.

Santiago Vidaurri in old age, probably in 1867.

Courtesy Museo de Historia, Castillo de Chapúltepec.

All involved realized that this was a serious matter. Quintero hurried to confer with Vidaurri, who insisted that he could not intervene in the internal affairs of Tamaulipas without incurring the wrath of its people and the federal government, for Juárez had recently removed him from the position of *comandante* in Tamaulipas. Finally, however, Vidaurri consented to write Juárez, Comonfort, and Manuel Doblado, his personal friend, then serving as minister of foreign affairs, to see if there were anything they could do to help. Vidaurri hoped that he would again be appointed military governor of the state in order to preserve the peace of the frontier.

Departing for Brownsville for an urgent conference with General Bee, Quintero met a messenger from Governor López who requested an interview in hope of settling the crisis. Quintero hastened to Matamoros where he immediately conferred with the governor. López presented a picture of helplessness. No state authorities were involved in the raids, he insisted. In fact, most of his troops were in Tampico and Mexico City, preparing for the French invasion; none were left to protect the Rio Grande villages. If documentation could be submitted proving that Pierce were implicated, López promised he would expel him. Meanwhile he granted the Confederate States permission to cross the border to pursue and punish the outlaws wherever they could be found.[65]

Quintero proceeded to Brownsville, where he discussed the problem of border security with General Bee. They concluded that the recent disturbances, plus the fact that Mexico had recently signed an extradition treaty with the United States, might create an atmosphere favorable to negotiation.

There were several problems to consider, the most important one being the peace along the border. Since the extradition treaty with the United States was not recognized in regard to the South, López proposed that the "principle of reciprocity . . . [be] ob-

---

daurri; *Boletín Oficial* (Monterrey), January 30, 1863; *Reports of the Committee of Investigation Sent in 1873 by the Mexican Government to the Frontier of Texas*, 66–67. See also the *Semi-Weekly News* (San Antonio), January 22, 1862, quoting the *Fort Brown Flag* (Brownsville).

[65] Quintero to Benjamin, Brownsville, January 30, 1863, in Pickett Papers.

served" with the Confederacy. He realized, of course, that two states could not sign an international treaty, but he explained that he was only being consistent with Mexico's federal policy by agreeing to extradition of murderers, thieves, arsonists, and the like. López and Bee openly agreed to work for better relations along the river. Secretly they concluded an agreement that stated: "Any person, who may commit the offence of murder, arson, embezzlement, robbery, cattle or horsestealing or larceny of chattles, personal property of the value of twenty dollars or more in either of the two States, and who shall escape to the other, shall be delivered over to the authorities of the place, where the offence was committed . . . ." They further agreed, according to Quintero, that fugitive slaves, a continual problem for Texas slave owners, would be extradited if they escaped into Tamaulipas.

These two "treaties," one public and the other secret, considerably improved the relations on the border, wrote Quintero. Unfortunately, he added, no captured document could be found in Pierce's handwriting, although his name was mentioned in one. The Mexican authorities would therefore take no action against the Union consul. In his defense, Pierce insisted that the marauders were simply trying to enhance their cause by implicating him. López, however, was probably unwilling to confront him anyway.[66] Thus the matter was settled peacefully, and López and Quintero apparently established more cordial relations as a result.

Another threat which Quintero had to regard realistically was that of an invasion by the Union army. He received reports as early as December, 1862, that an army under General Nathaniel P. Banks was preparing to invade Texas, intending to occupy the Rio Grande valley and sever the important trade routes.[67] This

[66] See extensive correspondence on this subject: Bee to López, Fort Brown, February 3, 18, López to Bee, Matamoros, February 11, 22, 23, Quintero to Benjamin, Brownsville, February 26, 1863, in Pickett Papers. See copies of both the public and secret treaties, and further related correspondence, in Letterbook: Official Correspondence between Governor Albino López of Tamaulipas and General H. P. Bee, C. S. A. Treaty of Extradition. Capture and Release of Col. E. J. Davis, U. S. A., 19–26, in the Confederate States of America Papers. López quote is from López to Bee, February 23 dispatch; treaty quote is from Letterbook, 20.

[67] Quintero to Benjamin, Monterrey, April 20, 1863, in Pickett Papers.

Monterrey, as seen from a housetop in the main plaza, to the west.

Courtesy Amon Carter Museum, Fort Worth.

also was rumored to be the goal of Yankee troops supposedly marching from Tucson, Arizona, to the Rio Grande. Describing his information as "reliable," Quintero explained the situation in his report to Benjamin and further stated that the expedition would include approximately 5,000 regulars plus New Mexico and Arizona volunteers. He noted that after it arrived on the border, however, Union men would flock to its banners, greatly increasing its size and potential threat. Supposedly the method of disrupting communications with Mexico would be the capture of the string of frontier forts stretching toward San Antonio. When the other force then landed from the Gulf, Quintero concluded, the two would combine to cut off Mexico from Texas.[68]

Another, more important aspect of Vidaurri's friendship was that he allowed trade between Mexico and the Confederacy. He and Quintero had established a rapport that enabled their two countries to engage in a very prosperous economic exchange. Wagon loads of goods crossed the Rio Grande from both north and south, carrying war materials, textiles, and foodstuffs into Texas, and cotton into Mexico. That Mexico was the largest outlet for Southern cotton soon became a significant economic factor for Texas in particular, but for the Confederacy as well.

[68] Ibid.

CHAPTER IV

THE AGE OF COTTON

The years between 1862 and 1864 were profitable ones for Governor Vidaurri. Under the protection of the Confederate diplomatic umbrella and his own efficient army, he engaged in numerous business activities with his son-in-law, Patricio Milmo, and collected healthy customs fees from the trade goods and cotton that passed through his domain en route either from Mexico or Europe to the Confederacy, or from the Confederacy to the outside world. The two men had established business houses in Monterrey, Matamoros, and several other cities along the border and had trusted connections at numerous other points. Although many items traveled through the area, cotton was still the most important. Vidaurri realized this and allowed it to flow unimpeded—so long as he got his profit from the trade.

The cotton trade into Monterrey eventually reached "enormous proportions," lamented the beleaguered Union Consul M. M. Kimmey, with "all kinds of army goods going back" into Texas.[1] The "trade is immense," declared Quintero. It "grows larger every day."[2] Late in 1864 a correspondent for the New York *Herald* wrote, "The Rio Grande trade has flourished ever since the blockade of the ports on the Gulf." Colonel Arthur J. L. Fremantle, while on a tour of northern Mexico, described "seventy vessels . . . constantly at anchor outside" Bagdad, with "their cotton cargoes being brought to them . . . by two small steamers." And

[1] Kimmey to Seward, Monterrey, October 29, November 21, 1862, in Monterrey Consular Despatches. Quotes are from October 29 and November 21 dispatches respectively.

[2] Quintero to Benjamin, Monterrey, September 24, 1862, January 25, 1864, in Pickett Papers. Quote is from January 25 dispatch.

"for an immense distance" along the shore he saw "endless bales of cotton."[3] The cotton trade had come of age and the economy of three states–Tamaulipas, Nuevo León y Coahuila, and Texas–depended upon it. Ships from several nations ignored the Union navy and hovered off Bagdad and Brazos Santiago, the port of Brownsville, awaiting their precious cargoes of "white gold."

Quintero had not waited for the resolution of the troublesome filibuster problems to take advantage of the numerous economic opportunities that were quickly becoming available. The British consul in Matamoros offered to allow any ships sailing from that port use of his flag. This permitted the Confederates to bring a steamer down the Rio Grande, place it under the protection of the British colors upon reaching Matamoros, then continue the journey. Still another method was the placement of Confederate vessels under the protection of the Mexican flag so that they could be used to unload the larger ships lying off the port.[4]

Regarding the war supplies that he had been instructed to contract for, Quintero reported that the firm of Oliver and Brothers in Monterrey was probably in the best position to supply the South. In addition to having a large capital and abundant resources, the company already had business contacts and considerable experience in Texas and New Orleans. To expedite matters, José Oliver proceeded to Richmond with various samples of products that his firm offered for sale: lead, delivered at Roma for $12.875 per 300 pounds; blankets, priced from $4 to $5 each; and shoes, sulphur, and saltpeter. The firm also had the capability of obtaining large amounts of small arms from England, Cuba, or perhaps the neighboring state of Zacatecas.[5] Upon delivery, the articles were to be paid for "cash down," although the brothers said they would also accept cotton.[6]

José Oliver was a hard bargainer and the Confederate officials

[3] New York *Herald*, January 9, 1865, p. 5; Kimmey to Seward, Monterrey, September 21, 1863, in Monterrey Consular Despatches; Fremantle, *Diary*, 6.
[4] Quintero to Hunter, Brownsville, October 18, 1861, in Pickett Papers.
[5] Quintero to Hunter, Monterrey, November 4, 11, 1861, and Quintero to Browne, Monterrey, November 6, 1861, in Pickett Papers; Quintero to Lubbock, Monterrey, November 9, December 2, 1861, in Governors' Letters.
[6] Quintero to Hunter, Monterrey, November 10, 1861, in Pickett Papers.

in Richmond could not reach an agreement with him. Even to Secretary of State Judah P. Benjamin he insisted that all goods that he supplied the Confederate States be paid for in advance with cash or cotton. Benjamin, of course, would agree to pay only upon receipt of the goods. Concluding that Oliver was "fearful of responsibilities" but realizing that he might eventually be of some use to the South, Benjamin recommended that the officials in Mexico keep in contact with him.[7]

Quintero, meanwhile, had made other agreements. Patricio Milmo contracted to sell flour to the Confederacy in September. On November 11, 1861, Quintero reported that since Oliver had left for the Southern capital, he had been able to obtain favorable rates on several important items in Monterrey. Rifle and cannon powder could be purchased elsewhere in Monterrey for $40 and $32 per pound respectively.[8]

Although he had reached no formal arrangement with the Confederate government when he was in Richmond, Oliver continued to sell supplies to individual purchasers in Mexico. The trade had become so intense that the firm had contracted for all the saltpeter to be had in Zacatecas and had sixty wagons operating between Monterrey and San Antonio. Lead, ammunition, saltpeter–*"everything with the exception of small arms"*–were included in the trade.[9] Blood, the Union consul, reported that there were even two powder factories fully active keeping the Southerners supplied.[10]

There was serious danger during the early months of the Civil War that speculators would move into the Mexican trade and raise the prices of necessary goods. As early as November 11,

[7] Benjamin to Mansfield Lovell, Richmond, March 22, 1862, in *War of the Rebellion*, Series I, Vol. VI, 863–864.

[8] Quintero to Hunter, Monterrey, November 11, 1861, and Milmo to [Quintero], Monterrey, n.d., in Quintero to Benjamin, Monterrey, December 23, 1863, in Pickett Papers.

[9] Quintero to Browne, Monterrey, February 9, 1862, and Quintero to Benjamin, Matamoros, July 5, 1862, in Pickett Papers. Quote is from February 9 dispatch.

[10] Blood to Seward, Washington, August 27, 1862, in Monterrey Consular Despatches.

Quintero had indicated that prices were rising and that the government should reach agreement with some suppliers while the prices were still reasonable. By December the price of saltpeter had risen two cents per pound. After apparently exhausting all sources for purchasing arms but still with no success, Quintero, on December 2, was offered approximately 370 rifles, muskets, and carbines, all in fairly good condition, for only $2,000. To prevent a speculator from obtaining them and realizing that there would not be time to get authority from Richmond, he wrote several of his Texas friends, including Governor Lubbock, encouraging them to make the purchase.[11]

Undoubtedly the most important commodity in the international trade was cotton. Cotton surely would have found its way into the Mexican market during the war. But after the Union blockade of Southern ports, which became effective on Texas ports in mid-1861, the simplest way for Confederates to get cotton out of the South was through Mexico.

In addition to the threat that Union fleets would seize the cotton, the Southerners encountered several other problems that they had to overcome before the exchange prospered. First, the political disturbances in Tamaulipas prohibited them from having free access to Matamoros to negotiate agreements for their crops. And, even if they had been able to deal with the Mexicans directly and immediately, there was no central coordinating body in the Confederacy. As later events revealed, simply too many agents were trying to deal for their clients or for their own cotton. Transportation also proved a troublesome obstacle. Although these might seem to be insurmountable blocks to the Mexican trade, Quintero, with the cooperation of Confederate authorities and Vidaurri, was able to aid in making Matamoros the "great thoroughfare" of the South,[12] the same thing "to the rebellion west of the

[11] Quintero to Hunter, Monterrey, November 11, December 2, 1861, in Pickett Papers; Quintero to Lubbock, Monterrey, December 2, 1861, in Governors' Letters.

[12] Pierce to Seward, Matamoros, March 1, 1862, in Matamoros Consular Despatches.

Mississippi . . . [that] New York . . . [was] to the United States."[13]

Heroic Matamoros, which had three times repulsed the American invasions during the Mexican War, very quickly succumbed to Confederate influence during the Civil War. Numerous residents already sympathized with the South, but economic interests brought even closer ties. Matamoros was actually "blocked up with goods," with no more storage space available.[14] The *Herald* correspondent described the increase in rent for both private houses and stores. In addition, he reported, there was a building boom, with "the carpenter and brick mason . . . busily engaged in erecting stores in every part of the city." Confederates themselves followed their cotton into Matamoros until they soon exercised some control as well as definite influence. In fact, during Christmas Eve, 1863, there were so many Southerners in Matamoros that they actually drowned out the Yankees aboard the off-shore blockading ships with "universal singing of Confederate songs, firing of guns [and] cheering."[15]

The cotton trade started slowly, but only because of the political difficulties in Tamaulipas. With Carvajal besieging Matamoros and the U.S.S. *Montgomery* manning the blockade off the coast of Brownsville, the Confederates could not reach the Gulf with their crop.[16] As Consul Pierce noted in March, 1862, the Southerners had a "large pile of cotton" on the wharves in Brownsville that they would ship as soon as possible.[17] The door was not completely closed, however. Until the political dispute in Tamaulipas was settled and Carvajal forced to stop his forays, much Confederate trade was channelled through Tampico, some 250 miles

[13] S. S. Brown to Lew Wallace, Baltimore, January 13, 1865, in *War of the Rebellion*, Series I, Vol. XLVIII, Pt. 1, pp. 512–513. See also Robert W. Delaney, "Matamoros, Port for Texas During the Civil War," *Southwestern Historical Quarterly*, LVIII (April, 1955), 473–478. Quote is from *War of the Rebellion*.

[14] William Watson, *The Adventures of a Blockade Runner: or, Trade in Time of War*, 24–26.

[15] New York *Herald*, January 9, 1865, p. 5; Commander J. H. Strong to Commodore H. H. Bell, off the Texas coast, December 28, 1863, in *Official Records of the Navies*, Series I, Vol. XX, 741.

[16] *La Bandera* (Brownsville), July 31, 1862.

[17] Pierce to Seward, Matamoros, March 1, 1862, in Matamoros Consular Despatches.

down the coast from Matamoros. The American consul there, Franklin Chase, considered the trade "gratifying evidence . . . [of] the efficiency of the blockade."[18]

Cotton seldom stimulated the economy of Tampico, however. Only when Matamoros was in the midst of a revolution, or when Union blockading vessels guarded it too closely, did the captains steer southward for the harbor on the Río Pánuco. The notorious blockade runner, William Watson, considered it an adequate alternative to Matamoros, though he was impressed neither with the shallow water, where a careless seaman might easily run aground or fail to navigate the "intricate channel," nor the attitude of the isolated citizenry, where the "arrival of a blockade runner always caused some stir." Difficult to locate because no prominent landmark existed at the mouth of the river and expensive because the larger vessels had to anchor at sea and unload by means of lighter boats, Tampico attracted very little attention from the merchants.[19]

Trade in Matamoros and Brownsville did not noticeably increase in the immediate aftermath of the Carvajal depredations, for by the time the political problems had been solved economic difficulties had arisen. The editor of the *Fort Brown Flag* lamented that "no transactions are taking place" because the "prices offer[ed] . . . and demanded are so wide apart." In addition, there was a two- or three-month supply of cotton already in Matamoros, and the river was so low that loading and unloading were considered hazardous. But even if there had been favorable conditions, the "want of steamboats under neutral flags add[ed] . . . to the embarrassment." As could be expected after a lapse in trade, expenses had increased because of the long delay, yet purchasers were not willing to pay inflated prices. Therefore, as the editor concluded, "There . . . [was] neither buyer nor seller" in the Brownsville market.[20] Carvajal's raids hampered the cotton trade to the extent that rumors swept Brownsville that the Union

[18] Chase to Seward, Tampico, August 6, 1861, in Despatches From United States Consuls in Tampico, 1824–1906: January 10, 1860–January 26, 1863.
[19] Watson, *Adventures of a Blockade Runner*, 125–126.
[20] *Fort Brown Flag* (Brownsville), April 17, 1862.

was going to withdraw the blockade momentarily so that some cotton could leave the port. According to the Brownsville newspaper, *La Bandera,* the "Doodles" needed the crop.[21]

One reason there was no more cotton in Matamoros was the inadequate transportation available. A railroad stretching from San Antonio to Brownsville, or even Rio Grande City, would have solved most of the problem. Regrettably there was none. The cotton had to be hauled by wagon from the principal market centers of Texas to the border towns. It was a difficult journey because much of the trip had to be made over semi-arid or desert country. Usually amounting to three cents or more paper money per pound, the freight cost (for 300 miles) to the Rio Grande often was as high as 50 percent of the value of the cotton itself, for two and one-half cents per pound specie was the market price. The price, of course, varied considerably, but even if the planter could afford the freight, that did not mean that there would necessarily be anyone willing to haul his cotton. Speculators, contractors, and the army employed most of the teams and drivers, because they could afford handsome prices or conscript the labor. To meet this challenge, Pryor Lea, the Texas agent in Brownsville, suggested that the primary route to the river be divided into three parts: from Alleyton (the end of the railroad) to Goliad, Goliad to the King Ranch, and the King Ranch to some navigable point on the Rio Grande such as Brownsville, Rio Grande City, or Roma. Lea wisely suggested that the planters could get the cotton to Alleyton, or perhaps Goliad, where Mexican teamsters could take it over the last two stretches of the route.[22]

John Warren Hunter, a youth of only fourteen when the Civil War started, graphically described the route from the King Ranch to Matamoros. "Ox trains, mule trains, and trains of Mexican carts, all laden with cotton coming from almost every town in

[21] *La Bandera* (Brownsville), July 31, 1862.
[22] LeRoy P. Graf, "Economic History of the Lower Rio Grande Valley, 1820–1875," II, 495–497; William T. Windham, "The Problem of Supply in the Trans-Mississippi Confederacy," *Journal of Southern History,* XXII (May, 1961), 162; James L. Nichols, *The Confederate Quartermaster in the Trans-Mississippi,* 8.

Texas," converged on Brownsville, he later recalled, making it
the "greatest shipping point in the South" and "Matamoros . . . a
great commercial center." Between the ranch and the border was a
"long stretch of 125 miles [which] became a broad thoroughfare
along which continuously moved two vast, unending trains of wagons; the one outward bound with cotton, the other homeward bound
with merchandise and army supplies."[23]

Other frequently used routes were even more desolate. One led
from central and western Texas through Austin, San Antonio, and
then on to Laredo or Eagle Pass. The other passed through Gon-
zalez en route to Laredo or Rio Grande City.[24] Mrs. Eliza Moore
McHatton Ripley, claiming to be one of the only women who
traveled the San Antonio to Laredo route during the war, described a scene she could not forget. Outside the Alamo City
she counted "hundreds of huge Chihuahua wagons . . . 'parked'
with military precision . . . waiting their turn to enter the grand
plaza, deliver their packages of goods, and load with cotton" for
the return trip to Mexico. Perhaps this was the most difficult
route to the border. It was "so barren that the only growths were
prickly-pear and mesquite," Mrs. Ripley wrote. "Rip" Ford, no
stranger to the borderland himself concurred in this judgment.
He found "hundreds of domestic animals, dead, their flesh seemingly dried up on their bones," around several of the water holes.
Following the scorching drought of 1863–1864 the situation worsened until L. M. Rogers, a friend of Ford's, claimed, "You cannot
imagine how desolate, barren, and desert-like this country is; not
a spear of grass, nor a green shrub, with nothing but moving clouds
of sand to be seen on these once green prairies."[25]

The ruggedness of the country complemented the rawness of
the men. Seventeen-year-old August Santleben, going to Mexico
"to seek . . . [his] fortune," encountered drought, outlaws, Union

[23] John Warren Hunter, "The Fall of Brownsville on the Rio Grande, November, 1863," 4–6.
[24] Charles W. Ramsdell, "The Texas State Military Board, 1862–1865,"
Southwestern Historical Quarterly, XXVII, (April, 1924), 265.
[25] Eliza Moore McHatton Ripley, *From Flag to Flag: A Woman's Adventures and Experiences in the South During the War, in Mexico, and in Cuba,*
81, 95–96; Ford, *Rip Ford's Texas,* 347–348.

refugees, and Confederate "sulkers" as he first freighted cotton from Columbus to Eagle Pass with an ox team, then worked in various cotton yards and factories in Tamaulipas and Coahuila. It was perhaps *Caballero Blanco,* Abram García, who struck the most fear in the hearts of the freighters and traders, Santleben felt, because of his "special delight in humiliating . . . [his] victims . . . by forcing them to dance at the muzzle of a six-shooter." Safety was never assured for the adventurers who engaged in the freighting business.[26]

After reaching a river port, the cotton then was loaded onto one of the many river steamers, which had been built especially for the Rio Grande traffic, and taken to Matamoros for transshipment to an ocean-going vessel in the Gulf.[27] The traffic was so enormous and the drought so prolonged that the city's dirt streets were "ground into a fine powder" several inches deep. Still, there were problems. Situated approximately thirty miles from the coast, Matamoros did not provide easy access to the sea. The port for Matamoros was Bagdad, a forsaken little village of almost 2,000 inhabitants in 1863, reachable by wagon, or by winding some sixty-five miles down the Rio Grande in a boat, a trip that easily consumed twelve hours, sometimes twenty-four.[28] Land transportation was also slow and expensive. Ox carts, two-wheeled wagons, and four-wheeled covered wagons carried most of the land commerce. Passengers rode in large coaches pulled by two or four horses or mules.[29] At least three stage lines operated between Bagdad and Matamoros by 1865: the Bartlett and Borge Stage Line, Kimbrough & Company, and the Bagdad and Matamoros Line.[30]

Before the war, Bagdad was an "unimportant little place, very

[26] August Santleben, *A Texas Pioneer: Early Staging and Overland Freighting Days on the Frontiers of Texas and Mexico,* ed. by I. D. Affleck, 22–35. Quotes are from pp. 22 and 32–33 respectively.

[27] Harbert Davenport, "Notes on Early Steamboating on the Rio Grande," *Southwestern Historical Quarterly,* XLIX (October, 1945), 286–289.

[28] Fremantle, *Diary,* 6–7. Quote is from Watson, *Adventures of a Blockade Runner,* 24–26.

[29] Neira Barragán, "El folklore en el noreste de México," 45.

[30] *Daily Ranchero* (Matamoros), June 11, 14, 27, 1865.

similar in appearance to other small Mexican towns"[31]–quite un-
impressive to most visitors. According to the correspondent for
the *Herald* "there were but two or three board shanties" in 1861.
But it soon changed. By 1864 "Bagdad [was] a full grown town,
with a population of not far from four thousand." It boasted
" 'first class' hotels, boarding houses, stores well filled with goods,
saloons and restaurants without number, and last, though not
least, a city police, which maintains order by night and by day."[32]
The "turbid, yellow waters of the Rio Grande"[33] had borne thousands of bales of cotton to this cluster of "miserable wooden
shanties."[34] Vessels of many nations, with "ropes of bananas inter-
mixed with yellow gourds" and "nets full of delicious oranges and
juicy pineapples" hanging from their rigging, waited in the Bagdad harbor for their cargoes.[35] Because of the Union blockade the
years of the cotton trade earned the description the "splendid
epoch" for this era in the states of Tamaulipas and Nuevo León
y Coahuila.[36] " 'Cotton is king,' in Matamoros and Bagdad," concluded the *Herald* correspondent, because "it gives them all the
vitality they possess."[37]

Even after the cotton reached Bagdad the trouble was not
over. It might be months before it could be loaded onto an ocean-
going vessel. Captain George G. Randolph, of H.M.S. *Orlando*, complained to his commander in January, 1863, that some thirty ships
were waiting for approximately 10,000 bales of cotton to be loaded,
because the steamboats used to transport the cotton from the
wharf to the ships could not cross the bar in the harbor if the
water level was too low. "It frequently requires from two to three

[31] Quote is from Max Baron von Alvensleben, *With Maximilian in Mexico:
From the Note-Book of a Mexican Officer*, 14. For further descriptions of
Bagdad, see William F. Hutchinson, *Life on the Texan Blockade*, 21; Watson,
Adventures of a Blockade Runner, 22.

[32] New York *Herald*, January 9, 1865, p. 5.

[33] Baron von Alvensleben, *With Maximilian*, 22.

[34] Fremantle, *Diary*, 6.

[35] Baron von Alvensleben, *With Maximilian*, 14.

[36] González, *Historia de Tamaulipas*, 79. Quote is from Roel, *Nuevo León*,
166–167.

[37] New York *Herald*, January 9, 1865, p. 5.

months to load a vessel," wrote Randolph. During the winter the tide allowed the shippers to work only about one day out of fourteen.[38]

Another of the problems that the Confederates had to face, and one that they did not handle satisfactorily until the war was already lost, was that of establishing a coordinating agency for cotton purchases and sales. As soon as the difficulties in Tamaulipas were over and Governor Vidaurri securely in control, swarms of Confederate contractors and purchasing agents crossed the border, and Mexican merchants and manufacturers sought agreements with Quintero. The New Orleans firm of Sandborn and Doen was one of the first to contract for Mexican goods, but it was followed quickly by merchants long involved in the border traffic. Charles Stillman as well as Wolf and Schwartz of Brownsville made deals in Monterrey and also in the interior. One Texas merchant took goods amounting to approximately $30,000 across the border in a long train. Soon Confederate agents from the Ordnance Bureau, George A. Giddings and Major J. F. Minter, were in Matamoros attempting to reach agreements with Mexican authorities for powder, uniforms, shoes, and stationery.[39]

There was little trust, no unity, and no cooperation in the Confederate effort. The entire endeavor suffered from waste, inefficiency, speculation, and competition among the Southerners. The "multiplicity of purchasers, speculators . . . competition and confusion," insisted Quintero, was "detrimental to the interests of the government." Actually the Richmond government hardly considered any trade with Mexico until the Union ships blockaded its ports; then it was too late to develop an efficient system.[40] The

[38] Randolph to [Commander Dunlop], January 1, 1863, in Foreign Office Papers, F.O. 50/378.

[39] Quintero to Hunter, Monterrey, February 1, Quintero to Browne, Brownsville, March 4, 1862, in Pickett Papers; Francis Richard Lubbock, *Six Decades in Texas: or, Memoirs of Francis Richard Lubbock, Governor of Texas in War-Time, 1861–63,* ed. by C. W. Raines, 360–369; Nichols, *Confederate Quartermaster,* 65–67.

[40] Quintero to Benjamin, Brownsville, January 30, 1863, in Pickett Papers; Graf, "Economic History of the Lower Rio Grande Valley," II, 492.

state of Texas was also lethargic. As early as January 11, 1862, the legislature had passed an act creating a State Military Board, primarily for the purpose of disposing of some United States government bonds that were left over from the Compromise of 1850. (The United States had paid the state of Texas $10,000,000 in bonds for the state to give up its claims to the land west of the present boundary between Texas and New Mexico. Texas had not yet cashed in all the bonds.) But in addition to bonds, the Board soon attempted to regulate any source of ready money, cotton being the most available.[41]

The control over cotton that the State Military Board exercised was somewhat duplicated by the Treasury and War departments of the Confederate government. Conflict was sure to come. The editor of the *Semi-Weekly News* in San Antonio lamented, "There are probably six hundred bales of cotton on the road from here to Victoria, which has [sic] been thrown off the wagons . . . because some Receiver or other officers thought it was being improperly sent out of the country." The situation was so bad that the honesty and intent of the government had been questioned by many planters, but the editor concluded that the main problem was "stupid officers" and "ill-advised and improper proceedings." "Many thousands of dollars worth of property has [sic] thus been lost to the owners and to the country by this stupidity," he charged.[42] Local generals also dispatched agents to purchase cotton. Apparently in an effort to obtain specie for his troops, the Confederate commander at Brownsville levied a duty of five dollars (specie) on each bale of cotton, for which he exchanged five dollars in Confederate notes.

With the establishment of martial law early in the war, the Southern government also required that permits be issued before cotton could be exported, hoping therefore to balance the imports and the exports. In this manner the government could withhold badly needed cotton until the South got the supplies that it so

[41] Ramsdell, "Texas State Military Board," 257–261; Lubbock, *Six Decades in Texas*, 360–369; Mitchell Smith, "The 'Neutral' Matamoros Trade, 1861–1865," *Southwest Review*, XXXVII (Autumn, 1952), 319–324.
[42] *Semi-Weekly News* (San Antonio), July 17, 1862.

desperately required. As might be expected, individualistic planters vehemently protested against the policy, feeling that the government was monopolizing the cotton business for generals and speculators. As a result, the order was repealed, and all military restrictions were removed from the Mexican trade.[43]

Although key circumstances—economic necessity plus the fact that Mexico was the only outlet—already favored a vigorous trade, Vidaurri improved them. When Quintero had requested it, he quickly lowered the tariff from two cents per pound to one. He also made Monterrey a "free depot" for cotton, meaning that any number of bales could be deposited there and left for perhaps a year, with a duty paid only upon shipment to Matamoros or toward the interior. The state of Nuevo León y Coahuila also had adapted itself to the new source of trade. It boasted eight cotton factories containing almost 14,500 spindles and 451 looms which could process 1,500,000 pounds annually. The Ibernia factory in Saltillo had 1,300 spindles and 40 looms, and consumed over 1,300 *quintals* of cotton annually. Employing some 180 workers, the factory produced approximately 11,500 "pieces of common brown sheeting called *manta*," which were sold to the Southerners for $4.50 each.[44] Quintero estimated that these factories could furnish enough clothing to supply all the slaves in Texas, and, if necessary, the rest of the Confederacy.[45] Vidaurri also opened up the river ports above Brownsville—Camargo, Mier, and Reynosa—and made them free ports of entry.[46]

For a brief time in July, 1862, Quintero feared that this happy arrangement might be destroyed when Juárez appointed General Comonfort as the new military *comandante* of Tamaulipas. Quintero asked Comonfort to decrease the duty by 50 percent, to one-half cent per pound, and he refused. But the general was sympathetic to the increased amount of international exchange and

[43] Graf, "Economic History of the Lower Rio Grande Valley," II, 499–502; Nichols, *Confederate Quartermaster*, 55.

[44] Lempriere, *Notes in Mexico*, 133.

[45] Quintero to Benjamin, Matamoros, August 14, 30, Monterrey, September 7, 1862, in Pickett Papers.

[46] Quintero to Browne, Monterrey, March 22, 1862, and Quintero to Benjamin, Matamoros, August 30, 1862, in Pickett Papers.

maintained the same tariff rates that Vidaurri had prescribed–
$5 per bale (500 pounds).[47]

In November, 1862, the new governor of Tamaulipas, Albino
López, a wealthy businessman and merchant himself, lowered
the duty on cotton to one cent from the one and one-half cents
that the previous governor, Juan B. Traconis, had imposed.[48]
Prices for cotton varied considerably but were still good enough
to attract trade. A rather expensive thirty cents specie per pound,
or sixty cents in Confederate currency, was demanded at Matamoros. Twenty cents was the price at Monterrey; closer to the
interior, in San Luis Potosí, a pound of cotton brought twenty-
six cents, and in Mexico City, thirty-five cents.[49] Under such
fortuitous circumstances the amount of trade stabilized and merchants prospered.

By mid-1863, although prices remained relatively stable–fifty
to sixty cents per pound Confederate money in Matamoros and
eighteen cents specie in Monterrey–the cotton exchange de-
creased considerably for several reasons. Farmers were unwilling
to sell for such prices, but the primary reason, Quintero wrote
in his report to Benjamin, was the lack of cooperation, coordination, and control among the Confederate authorities. The original
plan of the government was to trade cotton for essential war-
time goods, but, under an atmosphere of speculation and quick
profit, thousands of bales of Confederate cotton left Texas. No
essential goods came in for the people or the army. Quintero ad-
vised Benjamin that the government needed to control the cotton
market, not allowing any cotton to leave until the necessary
goods were available for trade. But he realized that under the
current circumstances this was highly unlikely, because the government was unwilling to pay the exorbitant prices demanded
by the planters. It was necessary, however, for the government
to get somehow the goods that it needed.[50]

[47] Quintero to Benjamin, Matamoros, July 5, August 14, 1862, in Pickett
Papers.
[48] Quintero to Benjamin, Monterrey, November 20, 1862, in Pickett Papers.
[49] Quintero to Benjamin, Monterrey, September 24, October 12, 1862, in
Pickett Papers.
[50] Quintero to Benjamin, Monterrey, June 19, 1863, in Pickett Papers.

Quintero hoped that by using its coercive power, the government would create a more favorable situation for the Confederacy. The price had declined in Matamoros because of speculation, something that Quintero insisted the market neither justified nor could afford. The Matamoros merchants, with healthy capitalization, were trying to make huge profits as middlemen. By refusing to buy, except at low prices, they hoped to force the market price down, as Quintero further explained to Benjamin, hurting their Texas friends. They speculated that the absence of cotton from the international trade would force the price up on the world market, thereby giving them a handsome gain. They simply wanted to buy low and sell high. Also to their advantage was the fact that the French had invaded and occupied much of Mexico already, shutting off such ports as Tampico and closing the interior markets, and forcing all exports from the north to exit through Matamoros. Unfortunately, Quintero saw little choice for the Southerners, but he did hope for better circumstances soon. His hope for change rested with the "small" dealers who were selling at from eighteen to twenty cents per pound. Their supply would be quickly exhausted, forcing them out of business and giving the large dealers and the government a monopoly. Then the Matamoros merchants would have to "call for it," that is, the demand for cotton would be so great that they would be forced to purchase it at the price the Southerners demanded. Also, because of an influx of specie from Europe, a number of new merchants would soon be in business and would break the hold that the establishment businessmen had on the trade.[51]

As Quintero specified in his report, the important issue remained governmental regulation of exports, and he offered several suggestions. He noted that the exchange of five dollars in Confederate notes for five dollars specie as a tax on each bale of cotton had been abandoned in February. The exchange, he insisted, was not such a bad practice, certainly not "burdensome" to the merchants, particularly since the government needed its

[51] Ibid.

specie to pay for goods and supplies bought in Mexico. The abolition of this tax placed another hardship on the government, because the planters and merchants could use the specie (not required for the tax) to outbid the government for the services of teamsters to deliver cotton to the border. Resumption of the tax would restore this advantage to the government as well as bring in a supply of specie to purchase material necessary for the war effort.

In addition, prompt and steady delivery of government cotton would cause the Mexicans to depend upon the government for trade rather than the merchants. The market price was high enough, Quintero continued, so that the five dollars specie should actually be a duty, rather than an exchange for Confederate currency. He speculated that this would supply enough money to support the entire armed force on the frontier, as well as give the government the badly needed control over the cotton market.[52]

One method the Confederacy adopted to help coordinate the shipment and sale of cotton was impressment. Agents offended a number of producers when they seized large amounts of cotton and quickly shipped them to Mexico. In fact, the inspector of customs at Eagle Pass, Jesse Sumpter, later claimed that the government demanded a "duty" of *one bale for each bale that went out of the country to Mexico.* As a result, several legal problems arose, only to be assuaged by Vidaurri's assurance that relations would continue undisturbed. Some of the Texans, upset at having their cotton impressed, traveled to Mexico in hopes of reclaiming it. The planters did not want to surrender their profits—perhaps even their livelihoods—so easily. One Texan followed his impressed cotton to Matamoros, where he stepped forward, produced the bill of sale which the Confederate officer had neglected to confiscate, and thanked the officer for helping him bring his produce across the river. The flabbergasted soldier had to stand by helplessly as the Mexican official investigated the document and declared that the cotton did indeed belong to the

[52] Ibid.

planter, because he possessed the proper papers. Vidaurri promised Quintero that he would support the Southern government, thus removing another possible conflict.[53]

Brownsville was the major outlet for cotton, but not the only one. In September, 1863, Confederate Major Simeon Hart, quartermaster at San Antonio, informed Quintero that cotton was accumulating in Eagle Pass because of inadequate transportation facilities and requested that Quintero acquire Mexican vessels for shipment. After approaching Vidaurri on the subject, Quintero reached a favorable agreement with him. Mexican boats would transport the cotton down-river to Matamoros. Ten percent of the tariff was due in Piedras Negras, the balance to be paid in Monterrey in Confederate drafts sixty days after delivery in Matamoros. Vidaurri reasoned that the arrangement would give the merchants time to dispose of their crops without being forced to accept the first price offered.[54]

While the economic pressure built up on the South, one firm, Oetling and Company, attempted to gain an advantage. A representative of the company offered a proposition to Major Charles Russell, quartermaster at Brownsville, whereby the major would profit personally if he aided the company in getting a large amount of cotton at a price far below market value. If he procured the cotton, Oetling then planned to deal with the government. In fact, he offered the Confederacy forty dollars in specie per bale of cotton under various possible arrangements. Twenty dollars would be paid in Alleyton or in New Orleans, and twenty dollars more per bale would be paid when the cotton arrived on the Rio Grande; or forty dollars per bale would be paid for the cotton at Eagle Pass, Rio Grande City, or Brownsville. In addition, Oetling was to pay all the freight charges and conclude European deals for the government. Major Russell favored the project (no doubt because of the personal gain involved). But

[53] Quintero to Benjamin, Monterrey, September 16, 1863, in Pickett Papers; Sumpter, *Paso del Águila*, 87; Watson, *Adventures of a Blockade Runner*, 28–30.

[54] Quintero to Benjamin, Monterrey, September 16, 1863, in Pickett Papers.

THE AGE OF COTTON

when the proposition was presented to him, Quintero vetoed it, claiming that better deals were available.[55]

Soon the market price changed upward, justifying Quintero's decision to wait. The increased number of merchants caused a supply shortage and therefore raised the price. Twenty-six cents per pound was the going rate in November, with not enough cotton available to fill the demand, yet Quintero reported to Benjamin that conditions might still improve. He expected the French to move in and capture Matamoros, with no effective resistance from Governor Vidaurri. Quintero felt that the bulk of the "present obnoxious duties" would then be removed, because the French favored freer trade with the South than did Vidaurri.[56] (The French were not as interested in economic gain as they were in political alliance; they would hope to influence the Confederacy by creating a favorable economic situation on the border.)

Trade goods coming from Mexico in exchange for cotton increased to include more arms and ammunition. In an opportunistic move, Quintero secured a large number of rifles for the South when the Mexican government was unable to pay for 40,000 stands of arms that it had ordered from New York. The customs officials in Matamoros offered them to Quintero, who eagerly accepted them. In order to insure that the shipment arrived, he suggested that the government notify the Confederate agent in Havana, so he could inform the French fleet not to confiscate the arms.[57] The supply of munitions seemed endless. Major Hart told General Henry Sibley not to worry about his supplies, because "we shall get all we want from Sonora."[58] Brigadier General Hamilton P. Bee considered the Mexican trade a "great advantage" for the South,[59] particularly after Major Hart contracted for

[55] Ibid.
[56] Quote in ibid.; Quintero to Benjamin, Monterrey, November 4, 1863, in Pickett Papers.
[57] Quintero to Browne, Monterrey, February 9, 1862, Quintero to Benjamin, Brownsville, March 1, 1863, in Pickett Papers.
[58] Hart to Sibley, El Paso, October 27, 1861, in *War of the Rebellion*, Series I, Vol. L, Pt. 1, p. 683.
[59] Bee to S. S. Anderson, San Antonio, November 30, 1862, in *War of the Rebellion*, Series I, Vol. XV, 882.

"over a million dollars worth" of material in less than two weeks in Mexico.[60]

Foodstuffs were also among the trade goods shipped from Mexico. Coffee, sugar, wheat, corn, and flour, all of which were badly needed, came with amazing regularity. According to the correspondent for the New York *Herald*, "The trade of this place . . . [is] supplying the rebels with all they need."[61] At least two large firms contracted with the Southerners to supply flour. Patricio Milmo and his partner, Evaristo Madero, signed an agreement in September, 1862; and L. Werlman, a Matamoros businessman, arranged to send 332 cargoes of flour to Texas if Vidaurri would but grant permission. Vidaurri apparently had no objection, even expressing regret that because of the unusually destructive drought then ravaging the country he could not send more grain as well. Quintero soon declared that all the flour needed by the South was now available in Mexico.[62] As late as December, 1862, he itemized large quantities of produce and breadstuffs on the market, including corn, but these foods soon became scarce. Flour, however, remained plentiful.[63]

Hoping to persuade the government to regulate trade between Mexico and the Confederacy, Quintero listed several incidents of duplication or mismanagement. A large number of purchasers and speculators increased the competition and chaos, which in turn increased prices and inefficiency for the South. In January, 1863, several agents appealed to Quintero for introductions in order to close various deals that they wanted. Although an agent from the Confederate War Department was in Matamoros purchasing over $1,000,000 worth of military stores, the Treasury Department and the Texas Military Board also had agents in Mexico

[60] Quintero to Benjamin, Brownsville, January 30, 1863, in Pickett Papers.

[61] New York *Herald*, September 17, 1863, p. 10; Quintero to Benjamin, Monterrey, September 7, November 20, 1862, in Pickett Papers; William Diamond, "Imports of the Confederate Government from Europe and Mexico," *Journal of Southern History*, VI (November, 1940), 489–499.

[62] Quintero to Benjamin, Monterrey, November 20, December 1, 1862, and Milmo to Quintero [Monterrey, December(?), 1863], in Pickett Papers.

[63] Quintero to Benjamin, Monterrey, December 1, 11, 1862, in Pickett Papers.

trying to market their cotton and bring supplies back into the South. In one instance, a Houston man asked for aid in securing transportation for his cotton, which was in the hands of both the government and private agents.[64]

There were even clearer cases of mismanagement. A shipment of some 15,000 "Enfield and Minnie" rifles was first delayed for a year then finally cancelled because of disorganized government agents. Quintero reported that the Belgian brig *Jane* arrived at an island off the coast of Honduras possibly without instructions. Regardless, the ship failed to deliver its cargo to the designated port, Brownsville. The brig anchored off the coast of Honduras for more than a year, having to sell some of the guns to pay expenses, then sailed without ever depositing the remainder with the Confederacy.[65]

In addition to poor coordination, other trade impediments had to be overcome. A prime obstacle was Mexican customs, which fluctuated according to whim and changed with the appointment of each new cacique. Vidaurri and Quintero presumably had reached a lasting settlement for cotton duty when an inspector from the central government arrived to put the Matamoros customs house "in order." Both Vidaurri and Comonfort, while successively serving a turn as military *comandante* of Tamaulipas, had agreed on a one cent per pound cotton duty. The federal inspector raised the tariff to one and one-half cents per pound, which, in Quintero's mind, equalized Piedras Negras with Matamoros as a port of entry. He wrote Benjamin that Piedras Negras should now develop more rapidly and would probably be open to the South, even if Brownsville were captured.[66]

Speculators and swindlers hovered near the border entry ports, many times acting with the aid of Mexican officials. Confederate Major Simeon Hart was swindled by a very simple method. He purchased a wagon train consisting of some 114 mules, 2 mares, and 4 horses from G. F. Justiniani, a Mexican citizen who had

[64] Quintero to Benjamin, Brownsville, January 30, 1863, in Pickett Papers.
[65] Ibid.
[66] Quintero to Benjamin, Matamoros, August 30, 1862, in Pickett Papers.

brought the train into Texas. Because it was loaded with goods, Justiniani had to pay a bond of some $272 to leave Mexico. After he sold the train to Hart, however, he returned to Piedras Negras and his bond money was returned by the customs collector, J. Jesús Silva. Then when Hart loaded the train with cotton and tried to recross the border he had to pay the bond, although it was a government train. Quintero suggested to Vidaurri that something should be done to discourage similar irregularities. Since Justiniani had a bank account in Monterrey, perhaps he should be made to pay the bond, Quintero concluded. Hart lost much more to another swindler, who got 600 percent profit on one of his shipments. This particular man's corrupt methods cost one Confederate officer his job.[67]

Later Quintero tried again to remove the duty from cotton, reasoning that it was taxed as if it were to be consumed in Mexico. Although failing to win his point, he reported to his superiors that the Southerners were actually paying considerably less than required by law, because Vidaurri had initially lowered the rate.[68]

Perhaps the tariff that the Mexican officials placed on goods coming into Texas was more troublesome, but Quintero had greater success in this endeavor. According to an agreement negotiated with Vidaurri, only 25 percent of the official rate was to be charged. But on October 12, 1862, under the new government of General Traconis, the rates were restored to their "old prohibitory" levels. Quintero protested, but Traconis explained his conviction that the Southerners should pay at least what the Mexicans had to pay. Texas, he felt, should not be favored over the states of Mexico. His ruling remained in effect until a weathy Matamoros merchant, Albino López, became governor in late 1862. He reinstated the 75 percent cut and promised that no new duties hampering international trade would again be levied.[69]

[67] Hart to Quintero, San Antonio, November 4, 1863, Quintero to [Vidaurri, Monterrey], November 20, 1863, Silva to Customs Collector Lorenzo Castro, Piedras Negras, October 27, 1863, in Expediente 343, Correspondencia de Vidaurri.

[68] Quintero to Benjamin, Matamoros, February 26, 1863, in Pickett Papers.

[69] Quintero to Benjamin, Monterrey, September 24, October 12, Matamoros, November 2, 1862, in Pickett Papers.

As if Quintero were not occupied enough fighting rate increases in Mexican customs, trouble came from a completely unexpected–yet controllable–source. Several Monterrey merchants complained to him that their cotton had been detained by order of General John B. Magruder at Eagle Pass and that their handwritten permits from General Bee went unrecognized. Magruder contended, according to the distressed merchants, that they had no contracts for the cotton. At a loss to explain Magruder's actions, Quintero appealed to his government for help, citing the fact that many of the Monterrey businessmen had entered the cotton trade at his request. If they were not given their cotton, he added, it would be the "death blow" to the commerce. Vidaurri, he insisted, had taken many measures to insure good relations and profitable trade for both sides. Understanding, Quintero continued, was the key–and in this instance a shortcoming–for the Confederacy. Even then the original confidence could be restored only with difficulty.[70]

Margruder probably stopped the trains because he was convinced the South lost money on each contract with the Mexicans. Even if the merchants had been requested to enter the trade, they had negotiated highly favorable contracts which Magruder felt should have been given instead to Confederate firms such as the one belonging to Richard King, Mifflin Kenedy, and Charles Stillman in Brownsville. He presumably intended to make sure the Mexican houses obeyed the law explicitly.[71]

These occurrences ranked as only minor incidents, however, when compared to the problems that arose in late 1863 and 1864. The menacing actions of the Union forces soon made Vidaurri an indispensable ally for the Confederacy—something the South would soon become for Vidaurri as a result of increasing pressure from Juárez. In early November, 1863, Union General Banks captured Brownsville, thus severing the Confederate trade routes to Matamoros. The seizure came as no surprise. Rumors to that ef-

---

[70] Quintero to Benjamin, Monterrey, March 21, 1863, in Pickett Papers.
[71] Magruder to General Samuel Cooper, Houston, June 8, 1863, in *War of the Rebellion,* Series I, Vol. XXVI, Pt. 2, pp. 57–65; Graf, "Economic History of the Lower Rio Grande Valley," II, 517.

SANTIAGO VIDAURRI

fect had circulated for months and many Confederates, no doubt, wondered why the Yankees had not come sooner. Realizing that if Brownsville fell his dispatches might be intercepted, Quintero had earlier prepared for such an eventuality by sending the key to a code to the State Department. The Southerners had correctly estimated the time of the Union invasion, for they evacuated the town, burning 600 bales of cotton and destroying army barracks as they withdrew. Many goods and much merchandise were moved to Matamoros. General Banks found a deserted city and took it without firing a shot.[72]

This is not to say that the capture of Brownsville was not a serious loss to the Confederacy. It was a vital link in the route to Matamoros. Near chaos reigned along the routes leading to the city. Confederate authorities attempted to warn teamsters to cross at Laredo or Eagle Pass, costly but safe detours.[73]

The situation radically changed in Matamoros, with conservative General José María Cobos showing his true loyalties. Following the Confederate evacuation, General Cobos, with approximately 200 men, crossed the river and occupied Brownsville until the Union troops arrived. Probably hoping to cement relations with Banks, he then returned to Matamoros, arrested new Governor Manuel Ruiz, and seized the city. As if according to plan, the famous Cortina joined him and became his troop commander. Nor was this situation to endure. Using Cobos's repudiation of the Juárez regime as the pretext, Cortina arrested and executed Cobos, then released Ruiz. Firmly in control, Cortina then informed Ruiz that Jesús de la Serna was the constitutional governor of Tamaulipas. Cortina planned to send Ruiz under escort to the interior, but Ruiz fled instead to Brownsville.[74]

[72] Quintero to Benjamin, Monterrey, November 4, 26, 1863, in Pickett Papers; Benjamin F. McIntyre, *Federals on the Frontier: The Diary of Benjamin F. McIntyre*, ed. by Nannie M. Tilley, 239–259.

[73] Hart to Confederate Secretary of War James A. Seddon, San Antonio, November 18, 1863, in *War of the Rebellion*, Series I, Vol. LIII, 913; Graf, "Economic History of the Lower Rio Grande Valley," II, 528.

[74] Quintero to Benjamin, Monterrey, November 26, 1863, in Pickett Papers; *Boletín Oficial*, November 15, 1863; McIntyre, *Federals on the Frontier,* 288–289.

Ruiz quickly organized an army in an ill-fated attempt to regain his governorship, but was soundly defeated by Cortina. And instead of Serna, Juárez, who had moved northward to Saltillo to escape the invading French army, appointed Cortina military *comandante,* and later governor, of Tamaulipas.[75] This meant that a pro-Juárez force was then in control of Matamoros, and, since the Confederates had cast their lot with Vidaurri, Brownsville was of little use, even after the Yankees withdrew and the Southerners reoccupied it.

Following the fall of Brownsville, the Confederates still had several Mexican ports of entry. Initially, trade was blocked because they did not know either the strength of General Banks's force or how far up river he intended to extend his control. But when it became obvious that Brownsville was his only goal, or at least the only one he could realistically hope to achieve, the Texans switched their trade routes to Laredo and Eagle Pass.[76] Mexican officials helped. Juan A. Zambrano, the customs collector at Matamoros ousted in the earlier *coup,* announced that all acts of the house since he had been deposed were illegal. Vidaurri stationed a large force at Piedras Negras, the most popular port of entry, to provide protection for the Confederate traders. Vidaurri's revenue from the customs at the Piedras Negras depot soon reached an estimated $40,000 to $50,000 per month. And from Eagle Pass, Sumpter, the customs collector, claimed that "scarcely a day [passed] that hundreds of bales [of cotton] were not unloaded" there. A "continuous stream of cotton wagons" passed through the border town headed for Mexico, some from as far away as Arkansas. One merchant, in fact, brought 100 wagons of cotton from Little Rock. The story in Laredo was similiar.[77]

---

[75] Quintero to Benjamin, Monterrey, January 25, 1864, in Pickett Papers; González, *Historia de Tamaulipas,* 86–90.

[76] *Tri-Weekly State Gazette* (Austin), December 23, 1863.

[77] Quintero to Benjamin, Monterrey, November 26, 1863, in Pickett Papers; Kimmey to Seward, Monterrey, February 28, 1864, in Monterrey Consular Despatches; *Boletín Oficial* (Monterrey), November 15, 1863; Sumpter, *Paso del Águila,* 87; Benavides to Vidaurri, Laredo, December 29, 1863, in Correspondencia de Vidaurri.

Even worse than the temporary occupation of Brownsville and consequent disruption of trade was the cessation of commerce in cotton precipitated by Patricio Milmo's seizure of a huge amount of Confederate funds–an action which Vidaurri condoned. The inability of Major Hart, quartermaster in San Antonio, to send cotton to Matamoros to repay Milmo, and the treachery of Major Charles Russell, the Confederate quartermaster in Brownsville, were primarily responsible. For various reasons it was a difficult task to ship cotton to Brownsville, and credit extended the South by Milmo increased to what he claimed amounted to hundreds of thousands of pounds of cotton. When Hart was able to ship some cotton to the port in partial payment of his debts, the vessel was apparently seized by Major Russell and applied to debts that he himself had accumulated.[78] Hart's bill not only went unpaid, but continually increased.

Hart's problem was further complicated by the disorganized method of gathering cotton used by the Confederacy. Much cotton that had been impressed went to other officers and other projects rather than to Major Hart in liquidation of the Milmo debt. Part of the problem was that the Southerners apparently lost between 600 and 800 bales when the Union invaded Brownsville. Hart speculated that the cotton eventually found its way into Milmo's hands, but he had no way of knowing. Moreover, Hart's agent in the Rio Grande valley, Peter Gallagher, was presumably implicated. Hart concluded that Gallagher had been acting recently "in the exclusive interest of Milmo & Co[mpany]."[79]

Milmo substantially inflated the total due him by taking over claims of several other companies such as Droege, Oetling and Company, and Attrill and Lacoste, as well as financing various agents such as A. Urbahan of San Antonio, who claimed that Hart owed him some half a million pounds of cotton. To com-

[78] Owsley, *King Cotton Diplomacy*, 125–126.

[79] See rather lengthy correspondence on this issue: Hart to Major George Williamson, San Antonio, December 24, 1863, Major George T. Howard to Hart, San Antonio, September 10, 1863, Hart to Milmo, San Antonio, November 17, 1863, and Hart to Williamson, San Antonio, December 28, 1863, in *War of the Rebellion*, Series I, Vol. LIII, 933–942. Quote is from Hart to Williamson, December 28 dispatch.

plicate the issue further, when the agents presented goods for sale to Hart and he refused them because of inflated prices, they would make a deal with Russell to deliver the goods–at the expensive rate–to Brownsville, even after that city was in the hands of the federal forces.[80] Clearly Russell was not working for the best interests of the South.

Then Clarence C. Thayer, the Confederate treasury agent, arrived in Matamoros on November 6, 1863, and unknowingly presented Milmo with an opportunity to seize his profits. Thayer was on a very important mission to relieve the money shortage in the Trans-Mississippi Department and to restore confidence in the government. He had with him seven cases full of Confederate notes totaling $16,000,000. Not knowing any contact in Matamoros, and noting the absence of the superior officer, he explained his mission to Major Russell, who claimed to be the ranking officer. He had a large amount of public funds that had to be delivered to San Antonio, he told Russell, but there was clear danger because the Union forces had already occupied Brownsville. Russell highly recommended Milmo and Company as being one upon which Thayer could "implicitly rely" because of its "good faith," and strongly urged that the money be placed in its care for shipment to Eagle Pass. Trusting Milmo primarily because of Russell's recommendation, but also because he was Vidaurri's relative, Thayer placed the seven cases in his hands to be shipped via Monterrey.[81]

Russell then left for Monterrey where he probably told Milmo the contents of the cases, thus prompting him to plan their seizure. On December 11 Milmo notified Major Hart that because of the huge debt that had accumulated, he was seizing the shipment and all the cotton either in Piedras Negras or en route. It was not until December 17 that he shocked Thayer by informing him that his shipment had been confiscated and was being held in lieu of the entire Confederate debt owed him, which was

[80] Owsley, *King Cotton Diplomacy*, 126.
[81] Quintero to Benjamin, Monterrey, December 23, 1863, in Pickett Papers. Quotes are from Thayer to Kirby Smith, Monterrey, December 20, 1863, in *War of the Rebellion*, Series I, Vol. LIII, 931–932.

greatly expanded as a result of Milmo's becoming assignee for other companies and agents.[82]

Upon being informed by Thayer of the seizure, Quintero immediately went to Milmo, asking that the cases be released. When the merchant refused to do so, Quintero conferred with Governor Vidaurri, requesting that he intervene on behalf of the South in the interest of preserving the commercial relationship between the two countries. Vidaurri promised to speak with Milmo, but later reported that his son-in-law was determined to hold onto the money and continue confiscating cotton until the debt had been paid in full. Apparently trying to convince Quintero of his objectivity in the matter, Vidaurri suggested that he might appeal the action in the courts if he so desired. Not feasible for several reasons, primarily the publicity that it would attract, this recourse was declined by Quintero. Quintero also was working within his own government to solve the crisis and requested that Major Hart do his best to settle the debt. Informing the State Department of his actions, he included the opinion that Vidaurri would also profit from the payment of the inflated debt and therefore favored Milmo's action.[83]

Milmo had listed a number of reasons for his seizure in his interview with Quintero. He had lost money, he declared, even in his first deal with the South. In September, 1862, he and Madero had contracted to exchange flour for cotton. Instead of being paid in cotton, however, he claimed that they were paid in Confederate notes, which had depreciated considerably and cost them money.[84] A similar situation provoked the confiscation.

[82] Quintero to Benjamin, Monterrey, December 23, 1863, and Quintero to Hart, Monterrey, December 20, 1863, in Pickett Papers; Thayer to Kirby Smith, Monterrey, December 20, 1863, and Milmo to Thayer, Monterrey, December 17, 1863, in *War of the Rebellion*, Series I, Vol. LIII, 931–933; Milmo to Hart, Monterrey, December 11, 1863, Milmo to [Quintero, December(?), 1863], Quintero to Vidaurri, Monterrey, December 17, 1863, in Expediente 343, Correspondencia de Vidaurri.

[83] Quintero to Benjamin, Monterrey, December 23, 1863, January 25, 1864, in Pickett Papers; Quintero to Vidaurri, Monterrey, December 17, 1863, in Correspondencia de Vidaurri.

[84] Milmo to [Quintero, December(?), 1863], in Correspondencia de Vidaurri.

A. Urbahan, Milmo's agent, had traveled to San Antonio to receive a shipment of cotton as agreed. But when he arrived, Major Hart claimed that he had none in San Antonio and offered 100 bales deposited in Alleyton. According to Milmo's instructions the agent was powerless to accept cotton anywhere other than in San Antonio, and he returned emptyhanded. In any case, 100 bales were far below the amount agreed upon.[85] Since the debt had continually increased, Hart apparently had made no effort to pay; Milmo therefore proceeded on his own.[86]

The Confederate response was swift and dramatic. Milmo was dealing with more than the interests of Major Hart of Texas. Because the Piedras Negras customs house constituted Governor Vidaurri's main source of revenue, Quintero suggested that if all shipments from Texas ceased, Vidaurri probably would be forced to capitulate and cause Milmo to release the cases. At least, he suggested, such an act might improve the climate for deliberations. Apparently the suggestion pleased the Confederate State Department. On January 12, 1864, General Edmund Kirby Smith, commander of the Trans-Mississippi Department, issued Special Order Number 8 forbidding any further shipment of cotton to Mexico. Kirby Smith improved upon Quintero's suggestion, because he also stipulated that all Mexican assets in Texas should be frozen until a final agreement had been reached. Then in a more conciliatory move, he appointed a commission consisting of Colonel Thomas F. McKinney, Judge Thomas J. Devine, and Captain Felix Ducayet, to go to Monterrey to negotiate a solution.[87]

[85] Milmo to Hart, Monterrey, December 11, 1863, in Correspondencia de Vidaurri.

[86] Milmo to Thayer, Monterrey, December 17, 1863, in *War of the Rebellion*, Series I, Vol. LIII, 933.

[87] Quintero to Benjamin, Monterrey, January 25, 1864, Quintero to Benjamin, Monterrey, February 1, 1864, in Pickett Papers. February 1 dispatch contains a copy of Special Order Number 8, Shreveport, Louisiana, January 12, 1864. See Kirby Smith to Vidaurri, Shreveport, January 12, 1864, W. J. Hutchins to Devine, Houston, January 21, 1864, copies in the Thomas Jefferson Devine Papers. See also Joseph Howard Parks, *General Edmund Kirby Smith, C. S. A.*, 302–305, 352–353.

Kirby Smith's instructions to his commissioners were explicit. First, they must "fully explain to Governor Vidaurri the precise nature of the steps" that he had taken regarding "Mexican property and the exportation of cotton." Second, they were to assure him that the Confederacy would repay the debt, yet they were also to "demand firmly the release and delivery" of the funds that Milmo held. They were "fully authorized" to represent the government's position in the matter and were to strive for a peaceful settlement.[88]

Vidaurri was under considerable pressure. With the cessation of cotton shipments, Quintero estimated that he would lose from $50,000 to $60,000 per month in customs revenue, his only income. Vidaurri had also alienated himself from the Juárez regime and had not yet committed himself to the conservative faction which demanded a monarchy. Juárez had recently moved his capital to Saltillo, and the French were expected momentarily in Matamoros. Vidaurri certainly did not want to lose the friendship of the South as well. Quintero expected that Governor Vidaurri would be forced to settle the matter peacefully.[89] Milmo and Madero were pressured even more when Madero's shipment was seized at Eagle Pass.[90]

Following Kirby Smith's action, results were quick in coming. The negotiation commission reached an agreement of which Quintero was uncritical. Milmo was to get 500 bales of cotton at Eagle Pass because he had substantiated his claim that the Confederacy owed him 500 to 600 bales at twenty cents per pound. In return for his liquidation of all items, damages, and interest from his claim, he was to get an additional 200 bales delivered in San Antonio. His partner, Madero, was awarded 1,500 bales, 500 to be delivered at Eagle Pass, 500 more on March 15 at San Antonio,

[88] Kirby Smith to [members of the commission], Shreveport, January [12], 1864, in War of the Rebellion, Series I, Vol. LIII, 949–950.

[89] Quintero to Benjamin, Monterrey, January 25, February 1, 1864, in Pickett Papers; Roeder, Juárez and His Mexico, II, 548; Flores Tapia, Coahuila, 129–130.

[90] Vidaurri to Kirby Smith, Monterrey, February 2, 1864, Manuel G. Rejón to Colonel Vicente Garza, Monterrey, February 2, 1864, copies in the Devine Papers.

and the final shipment to be delivered at some point along the Colorado or Brazos rivers as soon as practical. Milmo then released the $16,000,000 in Confederate notes that he had been holding, stopped seizing cotton, and resumed relations with the Confederacy.[91] Major Russell was ordered relieved of his position for his part in the affair.[92]

Vidaurri and the Confederates were thus back on friendly terms. They both had profited greatly from the cotton trade during 1862 and 1863. Nor were the trade arrangements between Mexican and Confederate merchants one-way affairs. In addition to Oliver and Brothers, one of the first firms to contact the Southerners, other large companies–Attrill and Lacoste; Droege, Oetling, and Company; K. Marks & Company; most with their headquarters in Monterrey or Matamoros–approached Quintero and reached agreements. The largest and most important company in the trade was Milmo's,[93] the company in which Vidaurri had a financial as well as personal interest.[94]

The most important item of exchange remained cotton. The foreign consuls in Monterrey strongly emphasized this fact when they informed Quintero that their government would furnish the South *"any amount* of specie" in exchange for the "white gold" at San Antonio, Eagle Pass, Roma, or Goliad. And, they continued, they could obtain approximately 500 wagons to put into the trade.[95]

The merchants quickly organized the trade. Kimmey, the Union consul, hastily informed his government that "large trains" were leaving daily carrying "goods of all kinds," that the "trade has

[91] Quintero to Benjamin, Monterrey, February 28, 1864, in Pickett Papers; [Devine] to Kirby Smith, Monterrey, February 24, Devine to Hart, San Antonio, July 25, 1864, copies in the Devine Papers.
[92] Endorsement on back of letter from Kirby Smith to President Davis, Shreveport, January 20, 1864, in *War of the Rebellion,* Series I, Vol. LIII, 930–931.
[93] Joseph Walsh to Secretary of State Lewis Cass, Monterrey, June 29, 1857, in Monterrey Consular Despatches.
[94] Ronnie C. Tyler (ed.), "Las reclamaciones de Patricio Milmo," *Humánitas,* X (1969), 561–583.
[95] Quintero to Benjamin, Monterrey, October 19, 1862, in Pickett Papers.

grown to be of great magnitude," and "it is difficult to say to what extent it may be carried or what proportions it may assume" if some action were not taken immediately.[96] Finally, General Edmund Kirby Smith admitted in mid-1863 that the Rio Grande was the "only channel" by which many goods could be introduced.[97]

An ideal economic and political situation existed during these relatively tranquil and prosperous years for Vidaurri. Secure in the governorship and a wealthy man besides, he could turn his attention to his city. In 1861 he had begun construction of the *alameda*, which was enlarged during later regimes. He also established the main plaza, the Plaza de la Llave, known then as "La Purísima," and began construction of the Mercado Colón, still one of the most popular tourist market spots in Monterrey. Vidaurri allowed Protestants—James Hickey from Ireland, Thomas N. Westrup from England, and R. P. Thompson of the American Bible Society—to begin missionary activities in Monterrey, perhaps because of the large influx of Americans during these years.[98]

Vidaurri continued to worry about such matters as the plans of President Juárez, the probability of a French intervention, and the possibility of having enough artillery and cavalry to protect himself in case of attack, but he had months to lay plans while he collected customs duties under the protection of Confederate diplomacy. Using the cotton trade, he gathered enough wealth to finance his army and maintain control of the northern states. The *caudillo* had been able to construct the ideal political situation for himself—a complete political vacuum in which he could be the dominant power. While opposing forces—the Union and the Confederacy, Juárez and the French—contested each other on various fronts, Vidaurri kept his balance in northern Mexico by playing one off against the other. This ideal political situation, however, soon vanished just as surely as it had existed.

[96] Kimmey to Seward, Monterrey, October 29, 1862, in *War of the Rebellion*, Series III, Vol. II, 949–950.

[97] Kirby Smith to Magruder, Shreveport, July 27, 1863, in *War of the Rebellion*, Series I, Vol. LIII, 885.

[98] Roel, *Nuevo León*, 166–167, 171–172; Sam Houston to Vidaurri, Austin, March 23, 1861, in Roel Papers.

CHAPTER V

THE END OF AN ERA

As a result of various circumstances beyond his control, Governor Vidaurri faced probably the most crucial decision of his political career in January, 1864. In his crusade for personal power, he had overcome uprisings, rebellions, and external threats, but one at a time. He was not sure that he could deal simultaneously with several threats to his power. As he surveyed the situation from the peaceful confines of his palace in Monterrey, he saw several possibilities. He could wait for the French to present their demands, but he felt sure they would occupy all the important cities of the north; the only way he could maintain his power, therefore, would be under French domination. Or he could confront President Juárez, who was certain to try to bring Monterrey into his sphere. Two such undesirable choices pleased Vidaurri not at all, and he soon proved himself either unwilling or unable to choose either alternative under the stress. He sat in Monterrey, virtually powerless to affect the outcome.

The factors dictating such an unattractive situation for Vidaurri, prompting the French intervention and his split with Juárez, rose from a complicated background. Juárez had had difficulty from the moment of his entry into the capital following the successful conclusion of the War of the Reform on January 1, 1861. He faced an uncooperative Congress that debated and stalled, offering few constructive suggestions to alleviate the problems. Fifty-one of the congressmen, in fact, signed a petition demanding that the President resign no sooner than he had entered the capital.[1] Nor had the country been completely pacified. Conser-

[1] Roeder, *Juárez and His Mexico*, I, 372–379.

vative General Leonardo Márquez roamed the countryside with his ragged band of guerrillas, and within a month had killed three outstanding liberals–Melchor Ocampo, Santos Degollado, and Leandro Valle. Dealing Juárez another severe blow, he ventured even to the outskirts of Mexico City before being thrown back by Porfirio Díaz, the liberal chieftain from Oaxaca.[2] A still more serious problem concerned the situation which induced the European intervention. Juárez had assumed control of a broken country, with necessary agricultural yield steadily decreasing, commerce almost nonexistent, and an unpaid army demanding its salary. He could pay neither the bureaucracy nor the foreign investors.[3]

The pretext used by European interventionists was Juárez's suspension of payments to foreign creditors on July 17, 1861. Although the country obviously could not meet its financial obligations, not everyone knew why. The British, in fact, were convinced that it was because of sloppy practices in the customs houses. Even after Foreign Minister Lord John Russell had solemnly affixed his signature to the London Convention along with representatives from Spain and France, Sir Charles Wyke, the British minister in Mexico, tried to guard Mexican sovereignty by taking over the customs receipts so Juárez could meet the foreign obligations.[4] The Mexican Congress, however, vetoed the plan (the so-called Wyke-Zamacona agreement), and the terms of the London Convention remained intact. The Europeans had pledged themselves to organize an expedition that would occupy the principal ports and military posts in Mexico. The only provision stipulated was that foreigners would be allowed to collect the debts due them, but there were at least two limiting clauses. Each country agreed neither to seek territory or private advantage nor to prevent the Mexicans from selecting their own form of government.[5]

[2] Ibid., 303–305, 313, 316, 318; Scholes, *Mexican Politics*, 69–72; Charles Allen Smart, *Viva Juárez! The Founder of Modern Mexico*, 254–255.
[3] Ernesto de la Torre Villar, *La intervención francesa y el triunfo de la República*, 83–92.
[4] Fuentes Mares, *Juárez y la intervención*, 67–74.
[5] Scholes, *Mexican Politics*, 80.

No sooner had the allied forces arrived than they promptly disagreed over goals. Spanish troops under General Juan Prim y Prats landed in Veracruz in December. English and French soldiers did not arrive until January, 1862.[6] Attempting to determine the exact nature of the demands that would be presented to the Mexican President, Wyke, Prim, and the French minister to Mexico, Dubois de Saligny, conferred in Veracruz on January 9. The French claims were extravagant. Saligny demanded 12,000,000 pesos in cash, full recognition of 15,000,000 pesos worth of Mexican bonds held by Swiss banker J. B. Jecker that the French had taken over, and even more. Realizing that nothing would have been left for their governments had the French demands been granted, Wyke and Prim were extremely upset with Saligny. But it soon became obvious that Saligny did not intend to be satisfied, that he was after something greater.[7]

The French had concocted a grand scheme—an attempt by Napoleon III to dazzle his listless subjects with a stimulating foreign policy. Such Mexican conservatives as José Manuel Hidalgo and José Miguel Gutiérrez de Estrada had convinced the emperor that the time was opportune for an invasion of their country. Starting with Mexico, Napoleon dreamed of creating another French empire in the New World. Consequently, Saligny's demands were not intended to be taken seriously, but were to serve only as an excuse for intervention, which the French promptly began.

In addition to the troops already there, another army under General Charles Ferdinand Latrille Lorencez arrived in Veracruz on March 6, 1862, considerably bolstering France's strength in Mexico. Protesting the violation of the London agreement, the British and Spaniards pulled out, leaving Mexico at the mercy of the remaining invaders.[8] Once General Márquez and his guerrillas joined Lorencez, they began their march on Mexico City, only to suffer an astounding defeat at the hands of General Ignacio

[6] Jack Autrey Dabbs, *The French Army in Mexico, 1861–1867: A Study in Military Government,* 19—20.
[7] Roeder, *Juárez and His Mexico,* II, 399—404.
[8] Ibid., 417, 423–424; Dabbs, *French Army in Mexico,* 22–24.

Zaragoza, Vidaurri's former officer, at Puebla on May 5, 1862.[9] A crucial battle because it boosted the morale of the Mexican troops, Puebla also convinced Napoleon to drop all pretenses of cooperation and thereby reveal his aggressive purposes.[10]

In Monterrey, meanwhile, Vidaurri watched the progress of the French armies with considerable interest, for he knew that very soon he would be forced to commit himself either to Juárez or to the invaders. The French "cause . . . seems to be gaining ground," Quintero observed in early September, 1862.[11] In fact, the French were approaching Puebla a second time, and it appeared that nothing could stop them this time.

More fully committed to the conquest, Napoleon sent General Elie Frédéric Forey and 30,000 veterans to Mexico in late 1862.[12] The very essence of methodic militarism, Forey took "heroic" Puebla de Zaragoza, renamed to memorialize its former defender who had succumbed to typhoid fever the preceding September. His victory came on May 16, 1863, after a siege of almost two months.[13] The fall of Puebla was a crushing defeat, squelching all optimism–and much hope–in the Juárez camp and sending them retreating toward San Luis Potosí in a "shameful flight." An escort of twenty-five men accompanied the dismayed President when he entered the city. "The government seems to be stunned with the blow," wrote Quintero to Benjamin.[14] The French troops continued their relentless advance. They crushed all resistance at Jalapa in November, causing various sympathizers to speculate that they would be in Sinaloa and Sonora soon and that their ultimate goal might be the Isthmus of Tehuantepec.[15] But they

[9] Colín Sánchez, *Zaragoza, evocación de un héroe,* 189–208.
[10] Roeder, *Juárez and His Mexico,* II, 457.
[11] Quintero to Benjamin, Monterrey, September 7, 1862, in Pickett Papers.
[12] Letter of General Forey, Veracruz, October 12, 1862, in Díaz, *Versión francesa,* III, 210.
[13] Fuentes Mares, *Juárez y la intervención,* 179; Roeder, *Juárez and His Mexico,* II, 495–510.
[14] Quintero to Benjamin, Monterrey, April 4, 14, June 1, 19, 1863, in Pickett Papers. Quote is from June 19 dispatch.
[15] Quintero to Benjamin, Monterrey, October 12, November 20, 1862, February 26, 1863, in Pickett Papers.

marched on Mexico City, encountering little or no opposition along the route. General Forey triumphantly entered the capital on June 10 and quickly began preparations for the Empire.[16] "The *liberal* party is fast dying away," Quintero warned Benjamin.[17]

Vidaurri somewhat naively hoped that he, Comonfort, and Doblado could form a government that could extract satisfactory terms from the French and avoid disruption of the country. Both Vidaurri and Comonfort had placed their hopes in Doblado, considering him either the ablest man or at least the one in the best position to act. He would be the president if they were able to form a new government.[18] But Vidaurri was also considering several other possible solutions. "In case . . . the war continued [and] some of the Mexican states . . . [proclaimed] their sovereignty," he told Quintero on May 31, Nuevo León y Coahuila "would be one of the first to do so." Refusing to submit himself to others, Vidaurri had already vetoed a league among Nuevo León y Coahuila, Tamaulipas, Zacatecas, and San Luis Potosí, proposed by the governor of San Luis Potosí.[19] Another alternative that he apparently did not seriously consider was offered by several prominent conservatives. Miguel Miramón and Benavides suggested forming a "national" party with Vidaurri as the leader. To this imaginative proposal, Vidaurri replied that he might consider it were it not for his ill health and old age. Quintero reported, however, that "the truth is that he does not rely much on these gentlemen."[20] Thus Vidaurri, alone and uncertain as to which course to pursue, waited for the French advance.

The French conquest continued unmercifully. Soon Vidaurri received verified reports that French ships stood watch off the coast of Matamoros, stopping some ships and confiscating various items. They did not want war supplies to reach the Juárez sympathizers who held Matamoros. Vidaurri guessed that both Mata-

[16] Letter of General Forey, México, July 7, 1863, in Díaz, *Versión francesa,* III, 249–251; Henry M. Flint, *Mexico Under Maximilian,* 37.

[17] Quintero to Benjamin, Monterrey, June 1, 1863, in Pickett Papers.

[18] Quintero to Benjamin, Monterrey, June 10, 1863, in Pickett Papers.

[19] Quintero to Benjamin, Monterrey, June 1, 1863, in Pickett Papers.

[20] Quote in ibid.; Quintero to Benjamin, Monterrey, February 26, 1863, in Pickett Papers.

moros and Tampico would soon be under French control and believed the only reason both had not already fallen was the yellow fever epidemic currently raging in both cities.[21]

Soon after the occupation of Mexico City, General Forey proceeded to stabilize French control. The young Austrian Hapsburg Maximilian had already been selected as the emperor, but he insisted that he be popularly "elected" before assuming his office. Forey dutifully supplied the desired plebiscite, and the Mexican commissioners hurried to Europe to convince the prince that his subjects eagerly awaited his arrival.[22] Creating a new government required the abolition of the old one. Forey, therefore, sent General Tomás Mejía to drive Juárez from San Luis Potosí, a task he easily accomplished in December. With all opposition fleeing before the powerful invasion machinery of France, Vidaurri had accustomed himself to the idea that they would be in Matamoros by the fall of the year. They were daily expected at various points in the north.[23]

Just how Vidaurri would react to the foreign incursions remained a mystery. He had not yet alienated Juárez, nor had he indicated that he would support the conservatives under the leadership of Juan N. Almonte, Santa Anna's old lieutenant, and welcome Maximilian. As early as July, 1863, however, Quintero suspected that he might lean toward the French because they appeared to have the best chance of winning. Vidaurri was appointed by Juárez as military *comandante* of Tamaulipas once again, and he sent approximately 3,000 troops to occupy Matamoros. The purpose, of course, was to defend the city as well as possible with the best army in the north. But Quintero suspected that, although he would send his troops to the port city, he would not "fire one single musket against the French."[24]

[21] Quintero to Benjamin, Monterrey, June 10, 1863, in Pickett Papers.

[22] Quintero to Benjamin, Monterrey, July 24, 1863, in Pickett Papers.

[23] Quintero to Benjamin, Monterrey, July 8, 16, 20, November 26, 1863, in Pickett Papers.

[24] Juárez to Vidaurri, San Luis Postosí, July 22, 1863, in Roel, *Correspondencia*, 203–204; Quintero to Benjamin, Monterrey, July 24, 1863, in Pickett Papers.

It soon became all too clear to the closest observers that Vidaurri was not sufficiently patriotic, nor was he sacrificing anything to help Juárez. Although his esteemed friend, Doblado, was appointed minister of state and foreign relations, Vidaurri persistently dissented from the policy of the Juárez administration. He favored, in fact, dissolution of the nation, and when that was rejected by Doblado, he withdrew his troops from the liberal command.[25] Undoubtedly aware that much potential support awaited their cause in Nuevo León, the conservatives sent A. Vigneau, the confidential agent of Almonte, to talk with Vidaurri. Attempting to instill confidence in the *caudillo,* Vigneau claimed that the French would capture Matamoros, thus cutting off the primary source of revenue from the *juaristas.* To encourage cooperation Almonte would send the governor arms, enabling him to repel the expected invasions by Juárez. The governor hesitated, but Quintero informed the Confederate State Department that "Vidaurri favors France."[26]

Vigneau did not intend, however, to invest all his hope for conquest of the north in the hands of Vidaurri. He proceeded to confer with Quintero, assuring him that the empire would not provoke a fight with the United States.[27] This point was highly significant to the Confederacy, for conflict with the Union would have allowed a blockade of the Mexican ports as well, thus eliminating the primary commercial outlet for the South.

After Juárez arrived in Saltillo on January 9, 1864, the massive French offensive ground on, engulfing San Luis Potosí. Vidaurri still expected Matamoros to be taken at any moment.[28] Yet he hesitated, clinging even yet to a forlorn desire to maintain his autonomous position in Nuevo León y Coahuila and unwilling to lend his support to the invaders or to the desperate defenders.

---

[25] Quintero to Benjamin, Monterrey, September 16, 1863, in Pickett Papers.

[26] Quintero to Benjamin, Monterrey, November 4, 9, 1863, in Pickett Papers. Quote is from coded statement in November 9 dispatch.

[27] Quintero to Benjamin, Monterrey, December 30, 1863, in Pickett Papers; José Fuentes Mares, *Juárez y el imperio,* 122.

[28] Quintero to Benjamin, Monterrey, December 30, 1863, January 25, 1864, in Pickett Papers.

Hoping to force him to join their ranks, the interventionists began printing items claiming that Vidaurri favored the conservative cause but that he was simply biding his time, waiting for a more advantageous moment to announce his support.[29]

In addition to the propaganda offensive, French General Achille François Bazaine drew nearer to Monterrey, increasing speculation that soon Vidaurri would either join the French or be deposed. On the other hand, Juárez had already indicated that he wanted to come to Monterrey, perhaps even establish his temporary capital there. Vidaurri found the thought of the President in Monterrey so distasteful that he used "every means in his power" to persuade Juárez otherwise.[30] Nevertheless, the vise began to close on the frontier governor, ending almost all hope of his retaining his traditional empire.

Although still definitely a challenge to Vidaurri, Juárez was in a weak position when he arrived in Saltillo. The extraordinary power that had been granted to him in order to conduct the civil war had expired, and, when he announced that he would appoint several new judges, General Doblado and General González Ortega objected, pointing out that the President no longer had such constitutional power. They then asked that he resign his office because of the violation. Shortly after Vidaurri learned of the President's arrival in Saltillo, he too sent a commission to request his resignation. Juárez steadfastly rejected the requests, but his position was weakened further as a result.[31]

Another source of constant anxiety to the President was government finance, irregular at best since the conclusion of the War of the Reform. Collections from Matamoros were inadequate, even when Juárez received them. The other alternative was the lucrative commerce that came through Piedras Negras and filled the treasury of Nuevo León y Coahuila—an estimated $40,000 to $50,000 per month. Shortly after the government located in Saltillo,

[29] See *El Pájaro Verde* (México), January 5, 11, 1864, quoting the *Courrier du Mexique* (Mexico City) in the January 5 issue.
[30] Quintero to Benjamin, Monterrey, June 22, 1863, in Pickett Papers.
[31] Pérez-Maldonado, "La pugna Juárez-Vidaurri," 58–59.

the minister of hacienda, José María Iglesias, reported to Vidaurri that the federal revenue was completely inadequate because of the French intervention, and that henceforth the customs receipts from Piedras Negras—perhaps as much as 600,000 pesos between June 1 and December 25, 1863—would go to the administration. Vidaurri, of course, protested that all the money collected was necessary for the maintenance of his state. The President, he added, should get his money from the port of Matamoros. Anticipating that Juárez might demand the Piedras Negras customs receipts, Vidaurri had ordered that they be given only to himself. On February 3 Iglesias demanded to know whether Vidaurri was going to obey the direct order from the President. While the governor was formulating an answer, presumably another herculean attempt at evasiveness, Juárez announced that he was proceeding to Monterrey.[32]

As Juárez continued his flight north, he realized that he might be confronted by hostile northern governors who had traditionally been virtually independent from the central government. Ignacio Pesqueira in Sonora, Luis Terrazas in Chihuahua, and certainly Vidaurri might easily choose not to support the President in an effort to maintain control of their states.[33] But Vidaurri was the crucial one. Juárez wavered in his decision to attempt the occupation of Monterrey because he could not anticipate Vidaurri's reaction. He had been discouraged from going to the city in previous contacts with the *caudillo* and consequently had grave reservations about Vidaurri's loyalty. In an effort to test the hospitality in Monterrey, he sent his son-in-law, Pedro Santacilia, ahead. Juárez was immensely relieved when he discovered that his wife had received a letter from Vidaurri welcoming her to his city with "most chivalrous cordiality." The *caudillo's* gesture con-

[32] Ibid., 59–68; Juárez to Vidaurri, Saltillo, February 9, 1864, in Roel, *Correspondencia,* 257; Quintero to Benjamin, Monterrey, January 25, 1864, in Pickett Papers; *Boletín Oficial,* February 9, 19, 1864; Santiago Roel, hijo, *El Cura de Tamajón,* [2]. Vidaurri may have already been in contact with the French. See Egon Caesar Corti, *Maximilian and Carlota of Mexico,* trans. and ed. by Catherine Alison Phillips, I, 306, 309.

[33] Rudolph F. Acuña, "Ignacio Pesqueira: Sonoran Caudillo," *Arizona and the West,* XII (Summer, 1970), 139–172.

siderably increased Juárez's expectations but did not completely befuddle his mind. Juárez wanted to use Vidaurri "for the good of the nation," but he had to decide: Vidaurri must either be "attracted or eliminated."[34] The fact that he favored the former did not mean that Vidaurri would actually be infected with the spirit of cooperation. After all, Vidaurri had not even wanted him in the state of Nuevo León y Coahuila and had so objected to his residence in Saltillo that he might easily have used arms against the President. Vidaurri clearly had an anti-Juárez record, ranging from incidents during the War of Reform, through harboring Comonfort in 1861, to the present situation.[35]

General Doblado, who had recently taken command of Juárez's army, preceded the President to Monterrey, no doubt to insure a peaceful reception. After a short delay in Santa Catarina, outside Monterrey, he and his 1,300 troops were joined by Juárez and his ministers before entering the city on February 12.[36] Although the *Ayuntamiento*, the city fathers, greeted the newly arrived dignitaries quietly, Vidaurri was nowhere to be seen. He had taken refuge in the *Ciudadela*, a fortress within the city, along with twenty-two pieces of artillery and a number of wagons, which he had tricked Doblado into giving him for safekeeping.[37]

On February 13 Vidaurri and Doblado met for a conference. Revealing almost childish sincerity, Doblado suggested that he might remain in the *Ciudadela* as a hostage while Vidaurri went for an interview with the President. He thought a face-to-face confrontation might be the simplest method of resolving the misunderstanding. Vidaurri was much more skeptical than his old friend. "Mr. Doblado," he reportedly asked, "are you so candid

[34] *El Pájaro Verde* (México), February 6, 1864. Quotes are from Roeder, *Juárez and His Mexico*, II, 547–548.
[35] Quintero to Benjamin, Monterrey, June 22, November 26, 1863, in Pickett Papers; Zamaçois, *Historia de Méjico*, XVI, 355.
[36] *Boletín Oficial Extraordinario* (Monterrey), February 12, 13, 1864; Quintero to Benjamin, Monterrey, February 28, 1864, in Pickett Papers; Pérez-Maldonado, "La pugna Juárez-Vidaurri," 68; Alessio Robles, *Monterrey*, 246–248.
[37] Quintero to Benjamin, Monterrey, February 28, 1864, in Pickett Papers; Pérez-Maldonado, "La punga Juárez-Vidaurri," 69–72; José P. Saldaña, *Historia y tradiciones de Monterrey*, 161–162.

as to pose the ruin of us both? My wife, who is no diplomat, but has natural prudence, tells me that this is absurd, because if the President shoots me and my men shoot you, Juárez will be the winner because he has gotten rid of both of us."[38] Doblado realized the logic of Vidaurri's statement and decided to withdraw from Monterrey, probably because he was convinced that he could win no military decision with the *norteños* ensconced in the *Ciudadela*.

Doblado's weak position became evident when Juárez and Vidaurri met for a conference the following day. The governor agreed to the interview only because he held the advantage. Knowing that Doblado's army was outside of town with no artillery and would be withdrawing shortly, Vidaurri feigned loyalty to the President and asked him to locate his government in Monterrey. Acceptance of the offer in reality would have meant domination of the national government by a state governor, for Juárez would have had no army in the city to enforce his decisions. But the pretense was soon revealed when Vidaurri's son drew his pistol and shouted that they should rebel. Juárez and his officials left immediately for Saltillo.[39]

Vidaurri, no doubt, was greatly relieved, for food was dwindling in the *Ciudadela,* and panic was spreading throughout the state because of the prospect of an armed conflict between the governor and the President. Probably in an attempt to calm the people and lead them to believe Vidaurri and Juárez were cooperating, Vidaurri insulted Juárez by publishing in the official state newspaper an account of the agreement with Doblado giving Vidaurri the President's artillery. The document revealed the stupidity of Doblado in approaching Monterrey and caused a slight rift between him and the President (Juárez could hardly afford to alienate Doblado and lose his support too). Vidaurri's earlier friendship with him probably blinded Doblado to the *caudillo's* traitorous path at this time.

[38] Sierra, *Juárez,* 421. See also *El Pájaro Verde* (México), February 17, 18, 19, 1864; Alessio Robles, *Monterrey,* 248–249.
[39] Prieto, *Lecciones de historia patria,* 503; Rafael de Zayas Enríquez, *Benito Juárez, su vida—su obra,* 189.

After they arrived in Saltillo, Juárez and his bureaucracy began their struggle against Vidaurri, whom they now considered a traitor. Hoping to secure the Piedras Negras customs duties upon his return to Saltillo, Juárez issued a decree on February 26 separating Nuevo León and Coahuila. A second order deposed Vidaurri from the governorship and declared Nuevo León to be in a state of open hostility against the nation.[40]

Quintero took advantage of the tense situation in Monterrey by conferring several times with Juárez. In fact, he was "on the eve of making private arrangements *with the President of the Republic,*" he reported, "in order to continue . . . [Confederate] trade through Camargo and Laredo." He had approached Juárez at a very propitious moment. The income from Matamoros was only a "small amount," Vidaurri had refused to contribute anything to the government, and the friendship of the United States seemed "to have turned into cold indifference." Quintero had a strong bargaining point, too, because the income derived from Southern commerce might well have become Juárez's largest source of revenue.[41]

Vidaurri realized that his influence was diminishing, for in addition to Juárez threatening invasion from the west, he received a letter from French General Bazaine on February 27. The "fratricidal war" was almost over with the armies of "ex-President Juárez" scattered and broken into small bands. The capitals of most of the states were in French hands. Now would be an excellent time for Vidaurri to aid in the "union of all the Mexican nation," which then would be "strong enough to defend her nationality." The decision was Vidaurri's. Opposite the peace which would be in the "true interests" of Mexico, there was war. And a

[40] *Boletín Oficial* (Monterrey), February 19, 1864; *El Pájaro Verde* (México), March 2, 3, 4, 1864; Pérez-Maldonado, "La pugna Juárez-Vidaurri," 71–75; Quintero to Benjamin, Monterrey, February 28, 1864, in Pickett Papers; Saldaña, *Historia y tradiciones,* 163–164; Kimmey to Seward, Monterrey, March 4, 1864, in Monterrey Consular Despatches.
[41] Quintero to Benjamin, Monterrey, February 1, 1864, in Pickett Papers; Quintero to Santacilia, Monterrey, January 29, 1864, in Tamayo, *Juárez: documentos,* VIII, 575–577. Quotes are from Pickett Papers.

struggle, concluded Bazaine, would be "disastrous" for Vidaurri.[42] Never one to make such responsible decisions openly, and always one to stall for time, Vidaurri replied that the decision was not his, that it rested with the people of Nuevo León y Coahuila, and he submitted it to a vote—war or peace, Juárez or the French.[43]

The presence of Juárez in Saltillo and the response to the French challenge considerably weakened Vidaurri's position with, and usefulness to, the Confederacy. Looking to what might happen in the near future, Quintero recommended the fortification of Eagle Pass. The Union forces could easily take Laredo should they decide to move out of Brownsville, and Eagle Pass would be the only remaining port of entry for Mexican goods. Under such circumstances, Vidaurri would be strongly tempted to close the Piedras Negras entrance in an effort to force the Southerners to support his rapidly fading cause. It would be reasonable, therefore, to station troops in Eagle Pass to prevent the closing of the entire border.[44]

But Vidaurri was to have no time either to contemplate closing the port of entry at Piedras Negras or to count the ballots in his referendum on war or peace. He had not yet reached a decision to support either the French or Juárez, probably because he wanted to wait until the last possible moment, then declare himself on the side of the likely winner. Had he intended to keep his domain in the north, Vidaurri would have been better situated at this time if he had openly declared his allegiance to the French and helped prosecute the war against Juárez. But he had already unknowingly made the choice. For when he decided to allow the people of Nuevo León to decide whom they would support, Juárez condemned him as a traitor—as if the interview in Monterrey had not been enough to classify him as a rebel against the legitimate government. Warned that Juárez was returning to

[42] Bazaine to Vidaurri, México, February 15, 1864, in *Boletín Oficial* (Monterrey), March 3, 1864.

[43] Quintero to Benjamin, Monterrey, February 28, 1864, in Pickett Papers; Vidaurri to Bazaine, Monterrey, March 1, 1864, in *Boletín Oficial* (Monterrey), March 3, 1864.

[44] Quintero to Benjamin, Monterrey, February 28, 1864, in Pickett Papers.

Monterrey with a stronger force, Vidaurri fled, abandoning any hopes he had that his government might survive the intervention intact. He also left his vast ranch in Coahuila and an interest in his son-in-law's business as well as other holdings. His interests now lay with the French.

Approximately 1,600 troops that Juárez had sent in pursuit overtook Vidaurri's force near Villa Aldama, approximately half-way between Monterrey and Laredo. The *norteños* surrendered and offered their services to the federal government.[45] But Vidaurri escaped. With the state archives and treasury, he crossed the Rio Grande near Laredo, spending a few days with his long-time friend, Confederate Colonel Santos Benavides.[46] Then he continued to Houston, where General John Bankhead Magruder welcomed him into one of the city's finest hotels.[47]

As soon as Vidaurri fled, President Juárez returned to Monterrey with his government on April 2, preceded by a force that numbered between 5,000 and 6,000 troops led by General Miguel Negrete. Negrete quickly laid the foundation for the establishment of the government by ordering the arrest of the lieutenant-governor and other functionaries who might still be loyal to Vidaurri, and by arresting Patricio Milmo on the charge of "being Gov[ernor] V[idaurri]'s partner in mercantile transactions."[48] When Juárez arrived on April 3, he began the tasks necessary to operate the government in Monterrey. The important customs port of Piedras Negras had already declared for him, and he sought loyalty statements from other municipalities. Supporting the measures that

[45] Quintero to Benjamin, Monterrey, March 8, 1864, in Pickett Papers; *El Pájaro Verde* (México), April 14, 15, 1864; William Marshall Anderson, *An American in Maximilian's Mexico, 1864–1866: The Diaries of William Marshall Anderson*, ed. by Ramón Eduardo Ruiz, 95–96; Kimmey to Seward, Monterrey, April 4, 1864, in Monterrey Consular Despatches.

[46] Benavides to Brigadier General James E. Slaughter, Laredo, April 10, 1864, in *War of the Rebellion*, Series I, Vol. LIII, 980–981; Kimmey to Seward, Monterrey, March 29, 1864, in Monterrey Consular Despatches.

[47] Houston *Daily Telegraph*, May 23, 1864.

[48] Quintero to Benjamin, Monterrey, April 3, 1864, in Pickett Papers; Milmo to British Foreign Office, Monterrey, April 22, 1864, in Foreign Office Papers, F.O. 50/383; *El Pájaro Verde* (México), April 25, 27, 1864. Quote is from Quintero dispatch.

Negrete had already taken to insure the approval of the citizens, he began publishing an official government newspaper, *La Opinión*, and his long-time confidant Guillermo Prieto started a weekly literary sheet of respectable poetry, romance, and satire, *El Cura de Tamajón.* The government remained in Monterrey for almost four and one-half months.[49]

Hoping to capitalize on his previous contact with Juárez, Quintero quickly built relations of a "friendly character" with the new authorities on the frontier. Juárez, too, seemed very interested in continuing the relationship, because he invited Quintero to dinner on the very day that he arrived.[50]

Meanwhile Milmo had been placed under arrest. This startled many residents of Nuevo León for he was a British citizen. He was jailed, although he protested his foreign citizenship, and finally paid a "fine" estimated at somewhere between $45,000 and $60,000 to obtain his release. The British consul supported his contention, and he was later sustained, but it was much easier for him to pay the amount and be released immediately rather than wait for the diplomatic processes to gain his freedom.[51]

Vidaurri's flight precipitated another incident which might have seriously endangered the lives of Quintero and the other Confederates in Mexico. In January Quintero learned of an alleged agreement between A. J. Hamilton, the Union Military Governor of Texas, and Serna and Cortina in Tamaulipas. Supposedly they had agreed upon the mutual extradition of "political offenders" that would include "any Confederates found in Matamoros." It was also disclosed that Serna and Cortina allegedly would seize any cotton in the city, sell it, and divide the

[49] *La Opinión* (Monterrey), April 21, 1864; Houston *Daily Telegraph*, April 16, 1864; Roel, hijo, *El Cura*, [3].
[50] *La Opinión* (Monterrey), May 5, 12, 1864; Quintero to Benjamin, Monterrey, April 3, 1864, in Pickett Papers. Quote is from Quintero dispatch.
[51] Milmo to the British Foreign Office, Monterrey, April 22, 1864, and Captain O. J. Jones to British Foreign Office, H.M.S. *Shannon* off the Rio Grande, July 18, 1864, in Foreign Office Papers, F.O. 50/383; Tyler, "Las reclamaciones de Patricio Milmo," 561–583; Houston *Daily Telegraph*, June 8, 1864.

money equally among themselves and Hamilton.[52] Such a deal probably never was made, but many people thought that it was because of various events that happened later.

As Vidaurri was preparing to desert Monterrey, his secretary, Manuel G. Rejón, left for Brownsville, intending to continue to Havana. When he reached Brownsville, however, United States Major General Francis J. Herron had him arrested. General Herron and Hamilton apparently fulfilled the terms of the rumored agreement when they transferred Rejón back into Mexico on March 27. On the following day he was shot–in the back, according to some accounts–as a traitor.[53] The Unionists next requested the arrest and extradition of Quintero, who was undoubtedly one of their primary enemies as one of the most effective Southern agents in Mexico. Fearing that he might indeed be surrendered to the Union authorities, Quintero, accompanied by Captain Ducayet, conferred with Juárez on April 6, asking whether the rumors that the government had entered into some kind of bargain with the Federals were true. Juárez, no doubt considering the revenue that he was already receiving from the Confederate trade, assured Quintero that Mexico had long had a heritage of granting political asylum, that both Unionists and Confederates were safe there, and that he would continue a neutral course.[54]

From the time of the interview until Juárez finally fled before the French on August 15, the commerce increased. In an effort to improve the trade further, Quintero asked former Kentucky Governor Charles S. Morehead who was in Monterrey en route to the Confederacy from Europe, to talk with the President. Governor Morehead readily undertook the task, attempting to keep open the exchange in lead, saltpeter, and sulphur. The Federals

[52] Quintero to Benjamin, Monterrey, January 25, 1864, in Pickett Papers.
[53] Quintero to Benjamin, Monterrey, April 7, 1864, in Pickett Papers; Houston *Daily Telegraph*, May 25, 1864; San Antonio *News*, June 18, 1864, quoting the *Union Journal* (Brownsville). For the Union reaction, see William L. Dayton to Seward, Paris, June 8, 1864, and Seward to Dayton, Washington, June 27, 1864, in "The Condition of Affairs in Mexico," *House Executive Documents*, 39th Cong., 1st Sess., Document No. 73, pp. 385–386, 390–391.
[54] Memorandum of the interview, Monterrey, May [sic] 6, 1864, in Quintero to Benjamin, April 7, 1864, in Pickett Papers.

were invoking various "sinister influences" to stop it. Apparently overcome with the glories of the Confederacy, Morehead did not speak of continuing trade relations with Mexico, but of the "certainty of ultimate success" of the South and of President Davis's friendship for the Mexican people instead. Juárez did again "promise to observe strict and impartial neutrality," but if Quintero was expecting further progress of commercial ties, he was disappointed. He did, nevertheless, remark in his report that "the commerce between Texas and Mexico is quite brisk," indicating that Juárez had no intention of severing the relationship.[55]

Even after the government seemed firmly established in Monterrey, Juárez encountered numerous problems that soon led him to withdraw. Although Vidaurri was finally out of the way, public faith in the President's leadership had not significantly increased. Zamacona, who had remained in Saltillo, wrote Juárez on June 16 that the empire, rather than Juárez, was now actually establishing peace and order. This, of course, bordered on treason. After an exchange of letters and with the disagreement becoming more obvious, the disillusioned bureaucrat finally requested that he be allowed to resign.[56] Later that same month, General Ramón Corona exposed the commander of the Army of the Center, General José López Uraga, as a traitor. Unable to conceal his position any longer, Uraga deserted to the French, taking a number of his fellow officers with him.[57] Disobeying a direct order from Juárez not to get involved in any major battles, General Doblado was defeated by Mejía at Matehuala, San Luis Potosí. He then went to the United States, ostensibly to negotiate with American officials, but actually caused Juárez "great concern" by assuring the Americans that he was prepared to cede territory for greater assistance.[58] Juárez had lost two of his better men.

To complicate the situation further, Colonel Quiroga, one of Vidaurri's most trusted officers, camped north of Monterrey along

[55] Memorandum, Monterrey, May 25, 1864, in Quintero to Benjamin, June 1, 1864, in Pickett Papers.
[56] Smart, *Viva Juárez!* 305.
[57] Scholes, *Mexican Politics*, 105–106.
[58] Smart, *Viva Juárez!* 308.

the Sabinas road with approximately 200 men, completely cutting off trade with Piedras Negras. Although apparently hostile, Quiroga disclosed that he wanted to fight for Juárez–but for pay. General González Ortega was sent to confer with him, but he returned disillusioned, for Quiroga had presented impossible demands, and González Ortega did not think the government should fight Quiroga with the French so near. Juárez thus began preparations to withdraw from Monterrey.[59]

The most important dispute during Juárez's brief tenure in Monterrey was with Governor Luis Terrazas of Chihuahua, who could have blocked his retreat. In this instance, customs receipts, conscription of men for the army, and difficulties over disposition of church property under the reform laws changed a misunderstanding into a protracted rift. Perhaps because of his experience with Vidaurri and his assumption that Terrazas was another selfish frontier *caudillo,* Juárez dealt rather harshly with him. In fact, the President sent General José María Patoni, governor of Durango, to depose Terrazas and install Jesús José Casavantes as the new state executive. Protesting his loyalty, Terrazas withdrew to El Paso del Notre while Juárez's appointees found their positions so unpopular that their accomplishments were severely limited.[60]

Juárez finally left Monterrey "amidst a shower of bullets" from Quiroga's guns. He struggled to reach Chihuahua, where the American consul, Ruben W. Creel, observed that citizens would afford him no "hearty assistance," and where the "Terrazas party . . . [was] working against him day and night."[61] When Juárez and his ministers arrived in the city on October 12 "worn out with fatigue and hunger," Creel reported that they did not receive any enthusiastic welcome. "I did not hear a single cry from the people

[59] *La Opinión* (Monterrey), July 14, 1864; Alessio Robles, *Monterrey,* 249–250; Smart, *Viva Juárez!* 308–309.

[60] Fuentes Mares, *Y México se refugió en el desierto,* 61–71, 81–90; Ruben W. Creel to Seward, Chihuahua, June 25, 1864, in Despatches From United States Consuls in Chihuahua, 1826–1906: August 18, 1826–December 31, 1869.

[61] Creel to Carleton, Chihuahua, September 18, 1864, in Chihuahua Consular Despatches.

in his favor nor in favor of the Republic."[62] Creel felt the President was a sympathetic, heroic, and unfortunate man, but surely the consul did not realize the validity of his prediction that the "misfortunes which attend[ed] the wandering steps of President Juárez . . . destined [him] to obtain historical notoriety."[63]

For approximately ten days Colonel Quiroga occupied the deserted city of Monterrey. Claiming to be the acting governor of the state by virtue of a decree that Vidaurri *"issued in Houston,"* he forced loans from the merchants. But his stay was short because of the approach of the French. When General Armard Alexandre Castagny occupied the Nuevo León capital on August 16, Quiroga fled northward to await Vidaurri's return. Attacking from the south, the French took Monterrey even before they reached Matamoros, but the port city also quickly fell to their power.[64]

The French occupation forced Quintero to renew negotiations to keep the frontier open to Southern cotton. He had been assured in March that the French would allow shipments of arms and ammunition to the Confederacy to continue, but he had to conclude the agreement with General Castagny. He expected success even though he noted that the French were "quite cautious and reserved in their intercourse."[65]

With intervention troops in control of both Monterrey and Matamoros, however, the societal situation changed radically. Captain Ducayet was a "distinguished guest" at a "grand ball" given in Monterrey in honor of the French, and was "entertained with great consideration" by several of Napoleon's officers.[66] After the social barriers had fallen, economic obstacles were next. With *"in transit"*

[62] Creel to Seward, Chihuahua, October 13, 1864, in Chihuahua Consular Despatches. See Florence C. Lister and Robert H. Lister, *Chihuahua: Storehouse of Storms*, 142–144, for a completely different description. See also Francisco R. Almada, *Resumen de historia del estado de Chihuahua*, 270.

[63] Creel to Seward, Chihuahua, October 10, 1864, in Chihuahua Consular Despatches.

[64] Quintero to Benjamin, Monterrey, September 5, 1864, in Pickett Papers; Vidaurri to Quiroga, Houston, May 30, 1864, in *Boletín Oficial* (Monterrey), August 18, 1864. Quote is from Quintero dispatch.

[65] Quintero to Benjamin, Monterrey, September 5, 1864, in Pickett Papers; Fuentes Mares, *Juárez y el imperio*, 122.

[66] Houston *Daily Telegraph*, October 1, 1864.

duties on cotton removed by Juan N. Almonte, General Castagny repealed the 25 percent "contribution" and the one dollar per bale duty, enabling Quintero to report happily that "we have never before been in such a favorable condition . . . in regard to our intercourse with Mexico." Honoring their earlier promise, the French allowed even the purchase of arms and ammunition provided it was done in a "quiet way."[67]

Trade continued to prosper until both France and the Confederacy were forced from their positions. Quintero described the French as having the "warmest feelings of friendship toward the Confederacy,"[68] inspired by the agreements reached in Paris between Napoleon III and John Slidell, the Confederate commissioner.[69] No doubt any arrangements calculated to aid the South politically or commercially could be made with the French.[70] "Goods come in as fast as possible," Quintero concluded in his last dispatch, because the "demand from Texas is extraordinary."[71]

In fact, the French made every effort to insure that the trade with Texas continued, for they needed the profit from the trade to help support their political conquest. After taking Monterrey and Piedras Negras, the French acknowledged what Vidaurri had known for several years: that Monterrey and Matamoros gave the more centrally located markets of Mexico "stiff competition" as a result of the Texas trade and poor communications with the rest of Mexico. "The population of the north would have been ruined," concluded *La Gaceta*, were it not for the commerce.[72]

Because of its vital importance, the French endeavored to keep the trade active as they continued their conquest of the northwestern portion of Mexico. They were worried in December, 1864, when over 6,000 bales of cotton were in danger of being lost in Piedras Negras because of a short-lived rebellion—which they hasti-

[67] Quintero to Benjamin, Monterrey, September 5, October 21, 1864, in Pickett Papers. Quotes are from October 21 dispatch.
[68] Quintero to Benjamin, Monterrey, November 5, 1864, in Pickett Papers.
[69] Owsley, *King Cotton Diplomacy*, 133, 507, 520, 522–523.
[70] Quintero to Benjamin, Monterrey, November 5, 1864, in Pickett Papers.
[71] Quintero to Benjamin, Monterrey, December 7, 1864, in Pickett Papers; Mauro, "L'economie du nord—est et la résistance à l'empire," 63–69.
[72] *La Gaceta* (Monterrey), November 9, 1864.

ly quelled–and when 500 bales were lost in a fire in Matamoros.[73] The French realized that the trade with the South was the only aspect of the northern conquest that was likely to be profitable for them economically.

Although the commercial ties across the Rio Grande were still vigorous and dynamic, neither party fared well militarily. In January, 1865, Castagny had to move his forces farther westward to control *juarista* guerrillas in Sonora and Sinaloa, leaving Colonel Pierre Jean Joseph Jeanningros in a temporary occupation of Monterrey.[74] Within a few months the city was once more in the hands of the *juaristas*. The situation on the Confederate side was considerably worse, with Union troops pressing the remaining Southern armies on every hand.

The Confederacy thrived a little longer in Mexico than it did in Richmond. Quintero left Monterrey soon after General Robert E. Lee agreed to surrender terms at Appomattox; he stayed for a while in Matamoros before moving on to Galveston to enter the newspaper profession again and work on the Texas *Almanac*.[75] But other Confederates were moving in the opposite direction. On his trek into Mexico, General Joseph O. Shelby found Monterrey filled with Confederates: former governors, ex-generals, miscellaneous officers, and numerous lesser figures.[76]

The Rio Grande trade had been essential to the war effort in the Trans-Mississippi Department.[77] John Warren Hunter later recalled that cases of Enfield rifles marked "hollow ware," gun powder barrels labeled "bean flour," and cargoes of percussion caps branded "canned goods" were shipped into Texas in large quantities. Confederate General John S. Marmaduke, in Little Rock, received a load of 4,000 Enfield rifles that had been purchased in England, then shipped through Bagdad, Matamoros, and Browns-

---

[73] Ibid., December 14, 21, 1864.

[74] Dabbs, *French Army in Mexico*, 99, 136, 141, 175.

[75] *Daily Ranchero* (Matamoros), May 24, 1865. The *Texas Almanac for 1868*, 60–64, 83–85, contains articles by Quintero.

[76] Edwin Adams Davis, *Fallen Guidon: The Forgotten Saga of General Jo Shelby's Confederate Command*, 99. For the story of Confederates in Mexico, see W. C. Nunn, *Escape From Reconstruction*.

[77] Richard D. Goff, *Confederate Supply*, 133–136.

ville, before reaching Little Rock.[78] Other items such as dry goods, hardware, foodstuffs, tobacco, and liquor came in through Matamoros. The South also tried to import military supplies and drugs.[79] At the height of the conflict General Kirby Smith admitted that the Rio Grande was the "only channel" through which the Confederacy could obtain many necessities. The trade was so extensive that several members of President Lincoln's cabinet–Secretary of the Treasury Salmon P. Chase, Postmaster General Montgomery Blair, and Secretary of State Seward–advocated the conquest of Texas, primarily to disrupt the Mexican trade. Secretary of the Navy Gideon Wells felt that a direct strike at Brownsville, perhaps even Matamoros if necessary, was the best course, but Seward vetoed that idea immediately, commenting that an attack on Mexico would involve the United States in a "war with the Lord knows who."[80] Brownsville did become a high priority objective, however. Still, the trade flourished until the war ended and Southern ports were reopened.

A sample of the cargoes actually confiscated by the Union blockading squadron suggested the variety and amount of goods shipped through Mexico. Copper, lead, arms, ammunition, powder, cloth, and flour were among the most important items that the South received. Although officially neutral and unwilling to penetrate the blockade, Great Britain exported large amounts of guns, ammunition, and material. From the schooner *Love Bird,* Yankees captured 14,200 Enfield rifles, 156 revolvers, 2,000,000 cartridges,

[78] Hunter, "Fall of Brownsville," 7–8.
[79] Frank E. Vandiver (ed.), *Confederate Blockade Running Through Bermuda, 1861–1865: Letters and Cargo Manifests,* 110, 130; Stuart L. Bernath, "Squall Across the Atlantic: The Peterhoff Episode," *Journal of Southern History,* XXXIV (August, 1968), 382–383; Bee to Anderson, San Antonio, November 30, 1862, in *War of the Rebellion,* Series I, Vol. XV, 882.
[80] Seward to Secretary of War E. M. Stanton, Washington, March 11, 1862, in *War of the Rebellion,* Series I, Vol. IX, 641; Kirby Smith to Magruder, Shreveport, July 27, 1863, in *War of the Rebellion,* Series I, Vol. LIII, 885; Avila Larios, "Brownsville-Matamoros: Confederate Lifeline," *Mid-America,* XL (April, 1958), 87; Ludwell H. Johnson, *Red River Campaign: Politics and Cotton in the Civil War,* 16–17; B. P. Gallaway (ed.), *The Dark Corner of the Confederacy: Accounts of Civil War Texas as Told by Contemporaries,* 109.

and 5,000,000 rifle caps. The *Gladiator* and the *Sea Queen* yielded 20,000 pounds of gunpowder, while 1,048 pounds of lead, boots, and spurs, percussion caps, gunpowder, and bird shot were taken from the *Sea Drift*. Union seamen removed 65,000 pounds of gunpowder, seven tons of horseshoes, and $4,000 to $5,000 worth of medical supplies from the *Flying Scud*. The blockaders also captured boots, shoes, steel, bar-iron, cloth, gold buttons, blankets, and even ready-made Confederate uniforms.[81]

One Confederate agent, Major J. F. Minter, purchased 5,000 reams of paper and stationery, over $1,000,000 worth of medical supplies, $15,000 worth of commissary stores, $1,300,000 worth of ordnance, and $30,000 worth of leather goods. In addition, he bought hundreds of thousands of pieces of clothing goods, rope, and bagging. The Confederate quartermaster at Brownsville reported shipping as much material to Alleyton and San Antonio.[82]

In return the Mexicans primarily imported cotton. The commerce was sufficiently profitable that both Vidaurri and Juárez accommodated the Confederacy, although neither of them particularly supported its goals. Even Napoleon III, recognizing the value of the exchange, allowed his officers to arrange favorable agreements with the Confederates, thus permitting the trade to continue. Undoubtedly Texas profited most from it, with few goods reaching the eastern bank of the Mississippi. It is a source of endless speculation, however, that a neutral Mexico, by selling valuable supplies and providing outlets to world markets, might have enabled the South to survive, had it been able to endure militarily.[83]

Perhaps one of the most lasting effects of the trade was the economic prosperity that accompanied it and remained to become the basis of financial empires on both sides of the river. Men in the cotton business accumulated "vast and immense fortunes," wrote John Warren Hunter. In Texas Richard King, Charles Stillman, Mifflin Kenedy, and others grew wealthy. On the Mexican

[81] Larios, "Brownsville-Matamoros," 71–72.
[82] Nichols, *Confederate Quartermaster*, 79–81.
[83] Samuel Bernard Thompson, *Confederate Purchasing Operations Abroad*, 125–126; Nichols, *Confederate Quartermaster*, 81–82.

side of the border, Patricio Milmo was perhaps the most notable. He lived until age seventy-five and by the time of his death in 1899, he had accumulated a large fortune estimated by various newspaper reporters to be between $10,000,000, and $15,000,000. Foreign merchants such as Droege, Oetling, and Company, profited greatly. Lieutenant Colonel Fremantle noted that "Mr. Oetling is supposed to have made a million of dollars for his firm by bold speculations" by 1863. Other merchants in Monterrey garnered profits that became the economic foundation of present-day Monterrey, the third largest city in Mexico and the financial capital of the north.[84]

Vidaurri's reliance upon the commerce was more direct. During 1863 and 1864, when Juárez occupied San Luis Potosí, his supporters controlled the nearby states of Tamaulipas, Durango, and Zacatecas, and the French threat severely limited possible action, Vidaurri relied on the South as his only ally. His income almost completely depended upon the revenue from the Piedras Negras depot, amounting to perhaps as much as $1,000,000 from 1862 until he fled in 1864. By the time the American Civil War ended, the Southern trade had wrought quite a change in northern Mexico. There was one textile mill—La Fama—in Nuevo León y Coahuila before the war started. By 1862 the number had increased, with other mills located in Coahuila and surrounding states. The main part of the economy of northern Mexico had been transformed to accommodate either the cotton industry or trade with the Confederacy.

But the Southern commerce failed Vidaurri just as King Cotton diplomacy failed the South. Quickly establishing an understanding with Juárez, Quintero negotiated favorable contracts and therefore the Confederacy did not have to help Vidaurri protect his stronghold. Just as France and England found it unnecessary to declare war on the Union to secure the thousands of bales of cot-

[84] Hunter, "Fall of Brownsville," 5; New York *Times*, February 18, 1899, p. 7; New York *Herald*, February 17, 18, 1899, pp. 12, 13, respectively; *Daily Express* (San Antonio), February 16, 1899, p. 5; Delaney, "Matamoros, Port for Texas," 486–487; Garduño García, *Nuevo León*, 40; Fremantle, *Diary*, 12.

152

THE END OF AN ERA

ton stacked on Southern wharves, the Confederacy found it unnecessary to fight President Juárez.[85]

Quintero may have been able to establish favorable trading relations without Vidaurri. But the fact remains that at the outset of the American Civil War, Vidaurri was a warm friend of the South when he was the major figure in northern Mexico, and Juárez at the same time was officially embracing neutrality, but openly cultivating the friendship of the Union. Perhaps Vidaurri can even be credited with the favorable commercial situation that existed in 1864 and 1865, for he had demonstrated to both Juárez and to the French that profit could be derived from trade with the Confederacy. In fact, he had so tuned the economy of his area to the Southern trade that his successors either had to accept the trade or recognize that Monterrey was the capital of a desert kingdom and relatively unprosperous. Vidaurri, in effect, forced his solution onto Juárez and the French by virtue of his success.

All hope had not died in Santiago Vidaurri's heart with the demise of the Confederacy. He carved a respectable career in the emperor's government in less than three years. Perhaps as planned, Vidaurri returned to Mexico from his Texas exile and he and Quiroga arrived in Monterrey on September 7, 1864. Having already recognized Maximilian as the rightful emperor, both were hoping that they would be restored to their positions of power in the north. Castagny, however, realized that Vidaurri represented a threat to French control of the frontier, and insisted that he continue his march.[86] Still together, Vidaurri and Quiroga arrived in Guanajuato where they offered their services to Maximilian and were accepted.[87] An extremely able man even yet, Vidaurri became a mainstay of the government, with Maximilian depending upon him for advice. Appointed a member of the Council of State in January, 1865, he survived a reorganization in October, 1866, indicating his growing influence. He still wanted to be placed in

[85] Thompson, *Confederate Purchasing,* 125.
[86] *La Gaceta* (Monterrey), September 7, 1864, contains Vidaurri's and Quiroga's statements, dated September 14. See also *La Gaceta,* September 11, 1864; Quintero to Benjamin, Monterrey, September 8, 1864, in Pickett Papers.
[87] Roel, *Nuevo León,* 178-179.

charge of his old domain, however, and cultivated several Republicans for the influence they could wield. But Bazaine and Jeanningros both suspected him of "double-dealing," and the minister of war, Juan de Dios Peza, accused him of being an insincere opportunist, so he was never able to return to Monterrey. When the Council of State met the following month, Vidaurri remained in favor, and after Maximilian and the imperialists were trapped in Querétaro early in 1867, he was named minister of finance and war. He faithfully discharged the duties of his office, quickly proving his budgetary skill by economizing "to the last peso." Although he cut the officers' salaries in half, he increased the morale of the soldiers by making sure that they were paid in full and on time.[88]

Vidaurri was with Maximilian in the final stand at Querétaro in March. He and Márquez were sent to Mexico City, Vidaurri to assume his duties as finance minister and Márquez to organize reinforcements to defend Querétaro at any cost. Vidaurri was also named to replace Teodosio Lares as president of the emperor's cabinet, and, if the emperor were killed, Vidaurri, Márquez, and José María Lacunza were to compose a regency to replace him.[89] Márquez, Vidaurri, and some 1,200 troops passed through the Republican siege lines and reached the capital. Upon organizing approximately 4,000 troops, Márquez turned to Puebla instead of Querétaro, which was beginning to "resemble a rat trap" in his eyes.[90]

Meanwhile Vidaurri set about raising some 300,000 pesos in order to relieve the desperate situation in Querétaro. Extremely unhappy because of his forcing loans—at which he was very adept by 1867—the wealthy complained, jeopardizing the small amount of stability that remained in Mexico City. Vidaurri wisely called for a conference with the editors of the newspapers and explained

[88] Luis Blasio, *Maximilian*, 138; Roel, *Correspondencia*, xvii–xviii; *La Gaceta de Monterrey*, February 5, 1865; Percy F. Martin, *Maximilian in Mexico: The Story of the French Intervention (1861–1867)*, 136. Quote is from Luis Blasio.

[89] Alberto María Carreño (ed.), *Archivo del General Porfirio Díaz*, III, 16.

[90] Smart, *Viva Juárez!* 377; Fuentes Mares, *Juárez y el imperio*, 222–223; Martin, *Maximilian*, 311. Quote is from Smart.

the extreme necessity, promising better treatment on the next occasion. His assurances somewhat relieved the situation, but Márquez's defeat by General Porfirio Díaz at Puebla caused further complications.[91]

The liberals were closing the trap, both in Querétaro and Mexico City. Márquez escaped back to the capital where he only disrupted the hectic cabinet meetings, causing Vidaurri to resign in disgust. Lacunza replaced him, but had no time to institute any policy because General Díaz surrounded the capital and all the imperial officers immediately went into hiding.[92] Upon learning of the executions of Maximilian, Mejía, and Miramón on the Hill of the Bell on June 19, Vidaurri sought refuge in the home of an American, James Wright, agreeing to pay him 5,000 pesos to keep quiet. He probably did not know that he had been sentenced to death as a traitor under the Act of January 25, 1862, but the illegality of the situation—he had not been present at any trial—would have offered no comfort at this point. Vidaurri was betrayed by Wright, apparently because he could not immediately pay all of the 5,000 pesos that Wright had demanded. Captured early in the morning on July 8, 1867, at number six San Camilo Street, Vidaurri was placed in a coach and shot without benefit of trial.[93]

Much has been made of the fact that Vidaurri was a traitor. His apologists have countered, saying that even though he was considered untrustworthy by Bazaine and Castagny, he remained loyal to and died for the empire. The most obvious demonstration of his consistency, however, does not seem to be his allegiance to Maximilian. The salient trait of his statesmanship is rather his steadfast devotion to his region and to the perpetuation of his influence there. He frequently failed to stand by the central government, from his refusal to participate in the *Plan de Ayutla*,

[91] Smart, *Viva Juárez!* 382.

[92] Hubert Howe Bancroft, *History of Mexico*, VI, 343; Greer, "Vidaurri and Juárez," 141.

[93] Díaz to Romero, July 9, 1864, in María Carreño, *Archivo del General Porfirio Díaz*, III, 123–124; James Slaughter to Milmo [México], July 10, 1867, in Roel, *Nuevo León*, 188–189; H. Montgomery Hyde, *Mexican Empire: The History of Maximilian and Carlota of Mexico*, 311; Zamaçois, *Historia de Méjico*, XVIII, 1651–1654.

through his withdrawal of troops from the liberal forces in 1859, to his clash with Juárez in 1864. But all were for the same reason: the extension of his power in his own region. Quintero strongly suspected–and probably correctly so–that the *caudillo* would have used the Confederate States to gain the final victory over Juárez had he been given the opportunity. Protection of his own sphere in Nuevo León y Coahuila again would have been the reason for his actions. His association with the French in September, 1864, is similarly explained: by allying himself with Maximilian he hoped to recover and again control his realm in northern Mexico.

Strictly interpreted, then, Vidaurri was a traitor–he did betray the trust placed in him by President Juárez and by the people of Nuevo León y Coahuila who remained loyal to the President. Juárez, in his flight from the French, had confronted the independently oriented governors of the northern states one by one, and all except Vidaurri had responded by officially declaring their loyalty to and support of Juárez. All had expressed their hopes for Mexican independence from European domination. Ultimately, Vidaurri stood alone in his public defiance of the President. In midnineteenth-century Mexico, unfortunately, Santiago Vidaurri was something of an anacronism. The hegira of Juárez had created a national consciousness, an awareness in which he could not participate.

BIBLIOGRAPHY

PRIMARY SOURCES

Manuscripts

Archivo Parroquial, Bautismos, Vols. I-III: 1700-1829. Lampazos, N. L., México. Microcopy, Rollo 696, in the Biblioteca Cervantina, Instituto Tecnológico y de Estudios Superiores de Monterrey, Monterrey, Nuevo León, México.

Circular letters signed by Vidaurri, August 14, 1843, June 25, 1844, March 17, 1845, in Western Americana Collection, Yale University Library, New Haven, Connecticut.

Correspondencia Particular de Don Santiago Vidaurri. Archivo General del Estado de Nuevo León, Monterrey. The papers are arranged alphabetically by names of correspondents. Expediente numbers are given for the documents that are filed under subjects rather than alphabetically.

Despatches From United States Consuls in Chihuahua, 1826-1906: August 18, 1826-December 31, 1869. General Records of the Department of State, Record Group 59, National Archives. Microcopy in the Austin College Library, Sherman, Texas.

Despatches From United States Consuls in Matamoros, 1826-1906: Vols. VII-IX, January 1, 1858-December 28, 1869. General Records of the Department of State, Record Group 59, National Archives. Microcopy in the Texas Christian University Library, Fort Worth.

Despatches From United States Consuls in Monterrey, Mexico, 1849-1906: Register, 1849-1906 and Vol. II, November 15, 1849-December 9, 1869. General Records of the Department of State, Record Group 59, National Archives. Microcopy in the Texas Christian University Library, Fort Worth.

Despatches From United States Consuls in Tampico, 1824-1906: January 10, 1860-January 26, 1863. General Records of the Department of State, Record Group 59, National Archives. Microcopy in the Texas Christian University Library, Fort Worth.

Devine, Thomas Jefferson, Papers. Archives, University of Texas, Austin.

Foreign Office Papers. 50/378, 50/383, and 97/516. Public Record Office, London.

Governors' Letters. Archives, Texas State Library, Austin.

Hunter, John Warren. "The Fall of Brownsville on the Rio Grande, November, 1863." Typescript in Biographical File, Barker Texas History Center, University of Texas, Austin.

Letterbook: Official Correspondence between Governor Albino López of Tamaulipas and General H. P. Bee, C. S. A. Treaty of Extradition. Capture and Release of Col. E. J. Davis, U. S. A., in the Confederate States of America Papers. Manuscripts Division, Library of Congress, Washington, D.C.

Notes From the Mexican Legation in the United States to the Department of State, 1821-1906: February 9, 1856-July 30, 1862. General Records of the Department of State, Record Group 59, National Archives. Microcopy in the Texas Christian University Library, Fort Worth.

Pickett, John T., Papers. Manuscripts Division, Library of Congress, Washington, D.C.

Roel, Santiago, Papers. Owned by Lic. Santiago Roel, hijo, Monterry, Nuevo León, México. Listed as "closed manuscripts," these private papers are closed to the public and were opened to the author only through the kindness of the owner.

PRINTED GOVERNMENT DOCUMENTS

Archivo Mexicano. Colección de leyes, decretos, circulares y otros documentos. México: Imprenta de Vicente García Torres, 1861. 6 vols.

Díaz, Lilia (ed.). *Versión francesa de México. Informes diplomáti-cos (1853–1867).* México: El Colegio de México, 1963–1966. 4 vols.

Gammel, H. P. N. (comp.). *The Laws of Texas, 1822–1897.* Austin: Gammel Book Company, 1898. 10 vols.

Manning, William R. (ed.). *Diplomatic Correspondence of the United States: Inter-American Affairs.* Washington: Carnegie Endowment for International Peace, 1932-1939. 12 vols.

Miller, Hunter (ed.). *Treaties and Other International Acts of the United States of America.* Washington: Government Printing Office, 1931-1948. 8 vols.

Official Records of the Union and Confederate Navies in the War of the Rebellion. Washington: Government Printing Office, 1894-1927. 31 vols.

Reports of the Committee of Investigation Sent in 1873 by the Mexican Government to the Frontier of Texas. New York: Baker and Godwin, 1875.

Richardson, James D. (ed.). *A Compilation of the Messages and Papers of the Confederacy, Including the Diplomatic Corres-pondence, 1861–1865.* Nashville: United States Publishing Com-pany, 1906. 2 vols.

U.S. Congress. *Congressional Globe,* Appendix, XXII, Pt. 2 (1849-1850).

———. *House Executive Documents,* 32nd Cong., 2nd Sess., Document No. 1, Pt. 2.

———. *House Executive Documents,* 32nd Cong., 2nd Sess., Document No. 54.

———. *House Executive Documents,* 39th Cong., 1st Sess., Document No. 73.

———. *Senate Executive Documents,* 45th Cong., 2nd Sess., Docu-ment No. 19.

———. *Journal of the Senate,* 31st Cong., 1st Sess.

The War of the Rebellion: A Compilation of the Official Records of the Union and Confederate Armies. Washington: Government Printing Office, 1880-1901. 130 vols.

NEWSPAPERS

Boletín Extraordinario. Monterrey. 1855 (Supplement to *Boletín Oficial*).

Boletín Oficial. Monterrey. 1855, 1857-1864.

Boletín Oficial Extraordinario. Monterrey. 1864 (Supplement to *Boletín Oficial*).

Daily National Intelligencer. Washington, D.C. 1855.

La Bandera. Brownsville. 1862.

Civilian Extra. Galveston. 1862.

Daily Express. San Antonio. 1899.

Daily Picayune. New Orleans. 1860, 1885.

Daily Ranchero. Matamoros. 1865.

Fort Brown Flag. Brownsville. 1862.

La Gaceta. Monterrey. 1864.

La Gaceta de Monterrey. 1865.

Houston *Daily Telegraph.* 1864.

New York *Herald.* 1863, 1865, 1899.

New York *Times.* 1899.

New York *Tribune.* n.d.

La Opinión. Monterrey. 1864.

El Pájaro Verde. México. 1864.

El Restaurador de la Libertad. Monterrey. 1855, 1857.

BIBLIOGRAPHY

San Antonio *Herald*. 1856.

San Antonio *News*. 1862-1864.

Segundo Boletín Oficial Extraordinario. Monterrey. 1855 (Supplement to *Boletín Oficial*).

Semi-Weekly News. San Antonio. 1862.

El Siglo Diez y Nueve. México. 1855.

Standard. Clarksville, Texas. 1854.

State Gazette. Austin. 1861.

Supplemento al número 2 del Restaurador de la Libertad. Monterrey. 1855.

Texas Republican. Marshall. 1861-1862.

Texas State Gazette. Austin. 1861, 1863.

Texas State Times. Austin. 1855.

Times-Picayune. New Orleans. 1937.

Tri-Weekly Civilian. Galveston. 1861-1862.

Tri-Weekly State Gazette. Austin. 1863.

Tyler *Reporter*. 1863.

La Voz de la Frontera. Monterrey. 1860.

Weekly Texas State Gazette. Austin. 1861.

BOOKS

Anderson, William Marshall. *An American in Maximilian's Mexico, 1864-1865: The Diaries of William Marshall Anderson*. Ed. by Ramón Eduardo Ruiz. San Marino: Huntington Library, 1959.

Baron von Alvensleben, Max. *With Maximilian in Mexico: From the Note-Book of a Mexican Officer*. London: Longmans, Green, and Company, 1867.

Flint, Henry M. *Mexico Under Maximilian*. Philadelphia: National Publishing Company, 1867.

Ford, John S. *Rip Ford's Texas*. Ed. by Stephen B. Oates. Austin: University of Texas Press, 1963.

Fremantle, Arthur James Lyon. *The Fremantle Diary: Being the Journal of Lieutenant Colonel Arthur James Lyon Fremantle, Coldstream Guards, on His Three Months in the Southern States*. Ed. by Walter Lord. Boston: Little, Brown, & Co., 1954.

Gallaway, B. P. (ed.). *The Dark Corner of the Confederacy: Accounts of Civil War Texas as Told by Contemporaries*. Dubuque: William C. Brown Book Company, 1968.

García, Genaro (ed.). *Documentos inéditos o muy raros para la historia de México*. México: Librería de la Vda. de Ch. Bouret, 1905-1911. 36 vols.

Hernández Rodríguez, Rosaura (ed.). *Ignacio Comonfort, trayectoria política. Documentos*. México: Universidad Nacional Autónoma de México, 1967.

Hutchinson, William F. *Life on the Texan Blockade*. Providence: Rhode Island Soldiers and Sailors Historical Society, 1883.

Iglesias, José María. *Revistas históricas sobre la intervención francesa en México*. México: Editorial Porrúa, S.A., 1966.

Lempriere, Charles. *Notes in Mexico in 1861 and 1862: Politically and Socially Considered*. London: Longman, Green, Longman, Roberts, and Green, 1862.

Lubbock, Francis Richard. *Six Decades in Texas: or, Memoirs of Francis Richard Lubbock, Governor of Texas in War-Time, 1861-63*. Ed. by C. W. Raines. Austin: Ben C. Jones & Company, 1900.

Luis Blasio, José. *Maximilian, Emperor of Mexico: Memoirs of His Private Secretary*. Trans. and ed. by Robert Hammond Murray. New Haven: Yale University Press, 1934.

BIBLIOGRAPHY

McIntyre, Benjamin F. *Federals on the Frontier: The Diary of Benjamin F. McIntyre.* Ed. by Nannie M. Tilley. Austin: University of Texas Press, 1963.

María Carreño, Alberto (ed.). *Archivo del General Porfirio Díaz.* México: Editorial "Elede," S. A., 1947. 3 vols.

North, Thomas. *Five Years in Texas: or, What You Did Not Hear During the War From January 1861 to January 1866. A Narrative of His Travels, Experiences, and Observations, in Texas and Mexico.* Cincinnati: Elm Street Printing Company, 1871.

Prieto, Guillermo. *Lecciones de historia patria escritas para los alumnos del colegio militar.* México: Secretaría de Fomento, 1893.

Puig Casauranc, José Manuel (ed.). *Archivos privados de D. Benito Juárez y D. Pedro Santacilia.* México: Secretaría de Educación Pública, 1928.

Ripley, Eliza Moore McHatton. *From Flag to Flag: A Woman's Adventures and Experiences in the South During the War, in Mexico, and in Cuba.* New York: D. Appleton and Company, 1889.

Roel, Santiago (ed.). *Correspondencia particular de D. Santiago Vidaurri, gobernador de Nuevo León (1855-1864).* Monterrey: Universidad de Nuevo León, 1946.

Roel, Santiago, hijo. *El Cura de Tamajón.* Monterrey: Gobierno del Estado de Nuevo León, 1967.

Santleben, August. *A Texas Pioneer: Early Staging and Overland Freighting Days on the Frontiers of Texas and Mexico.* Ed. by I. D. Affleck. New York: Neale Publishing Company, 1910.

Sumpter, Jesse. *Paso del Águila: A Chronicle of Frontier Days on the Texas Border.* Ed. by Ben E. Pingenot. Austin: The Encino Press, 1969.

Tamayo, Jorge L. (ed.). *Benito Juárez: documentos, discursos y correspondencia.* México: Secretaría del Patrimonio Nacional, 1964-1966. 9 vols.

Torre Villar, Ernesto de la. *La intervención francesa y el triunfo de la República*. México: Fondo de Cultura Económica, 1968.

————— (ed.) *El Triunfo de la república liberal, 1857-1860*. México: Fondo de Cultura Económica, 1960.

Vandiver, Frank E. (ed.). *Confederate Blockade Running Through Bermuda, 1861-1865: Letters and Cargo Manifests*. Austin: University of Texas Press, 1947.

Watson, William. *The Adventures of a Blockade Runner: or, Trade in Time of War*. London: T. Fisher Unwin, 1892.

Williams, Amelia W., and Barker, Eugene C. (eds.). *The Writings of Sam Houston*. Austin: University of Texas Press, 1939-1943. 8 vols.

ARTICLES

Faulk, Odie B. (ed.). "Projected Mexican Colonies in the Borderlands, 1852," *Journal of Arizona History*, X (Summer, 1969), 115-128.

Moseley, Edward H. (ed.). "Documents—A Witness for the Prosecution: The Pickett Incident," *The Register of the Kentucky Historical Society*, LXVIII (April, 1970), 171–179.

Pérez-Maldonado, Carlos (ed.). "La pugna Juárez-Vidaurri en Monterrey–1864," *Memorias de la Academia Mexicana de la Historia, XXIV* (enero-marzo, 1965), 56–91.

Tyler, Ronnie C. (ed.). "Las reclamaciones de Patricio Milmo," *Humánitas*, X (1969), 561–583.

SECONDARY SOURCES

BOOKS

Alessio Robles, Vito. *Monterrey en la historia y en la leyenda*. México: Antigua Librería Robredo de José Porrúa e Hijos, 1936.

Almada, Francisco R. *Resumen de historia del estado de Chihua-hua*. México: Libros Mexicanos, 1955.

Bancroft, Hubert Howe. *History of Mexico*. San Francisco: A. L. Bancroft & Company, 1883-1888. 6 vols.

————. *History of the North Mexican States and Texas*. San Francisco: A. L. Bancroft & Company, 1884-1889. 2 vols.

Berrueto Ramón, Federico. *Ignacio Zaragoza*. México: Secretaría de Gobernación, 1962.

Callahan, James M. *American Foreign Policy in Mexican Relations*. New York: The Macmillan Company, 1932.

————. *The Diplomatic History of the Southern Confederation*. Baltimore: Johns Hopkins Press, 1901.

Callcott, Wilfred H. *Church and State in Mexico, 1822-1857*. Durham: Duke University Press, 1926.

Carbonell, José Manuel. *Las poetas de "El Laud del Desterrado."* Havana: Imprenta Advisador Comercial, 1930.

Castellanos García, Gerardo. *Panorama histórico; esayo de crono-logía cubana, desde 1492 hasta 1933*. La Habana: Ucar, García y Cia., 1934.

Cavazos Garza, Israel. *El Colegio Civil de Nuevo León: para su historia*. Monterrey: Universidad de Nuevo León, 1957.

Colín Sánchez, Guillermo. *Ignacio Zaragoza, evocación de un héroe*. México: Editorial Porrúa, S.A., 1963.

Corti, Egon Caesar. *Maximilian and Carlota of Mexico*. Trans. and ed. by Catherine Alison Phillips. New York: Alfred A. Knopf, 1928. 2 vols.

Cuba en la mano; enciclopedia popular ilustrada. La Habana: Ucar, García y Cia., 1940.

Dabbs, Jack Autrey. *The French Army in Mexico, 1861-1867*: A *Study in Military Government*. The Hague: Mouton and Company, 1963.

Davis, Edwin Adams. *Fallen Guidon: The Forgotten Saga of General Jo Shelby's Confederate Command*. Santa Fe: Stagecoach Press, 1962.

[Elías Hernández, José]. *El Laud del Desterrado*. New York: Imprenta de "La Revolucion," 1858.

Flores Tapia, Oscar. *Coahuila: la reforma, la intervención y el imperio*. Saltillo: Talleres Gráficos del Gobierno del Estado, 1966.

Friend, Llerena. *Sam Houston, the Great Designer*. Austin: University of Texas Press, 1954.

Fuentes Díaz, Vicente. *Santos Degollado, el santo de la reforma*. México: Talleres Imprenta Arana, S.A., 1959.

Fuentes Mares, José. *Juárez y el imperio*. México: Editorial Jus, 1963.

———. *Juárez y la intervención*. México: Editorial Jus, 1962.

———. *Y México se refugió en el desierto; Luis Terrazas: historia y destino*. México: Editorial Jus, 1954.

Garduño García, Horacio. *Nuevo León, un ejemplo de protección a la industria de transformación*. México: Universidad Nacional Autónoma de México, 1958.

Goff, Richard D. *Confederate Supply*. Durham: Duke University Press, 1969.

González, Arturo. *Historia de Tamaulipas*. Ciudad Victoria: Biblioteca "El Lápiz Rojo," 1931.

Hale, Charles A. *Mexican Liberalism in the Age of Mora, 1821-1853*. New Haven: Yale University Press, 1968.

Hall, Martin Hardwick. *Sibley's New Mexico Campaign*. Austin: University of Texas Press, 1960.

Hendrick, Burton J. *Statesmen of the Lost Cause: Jefferson Davis and His Cabinet.* Boston: Little, Brown & Company, 1939.

Hernández Millares, Jorge, and Carrillo Escribano, Alejandro. *Atlas Porrúa de la República Mexicana.* México: Editorial Porrúa, S.A., 1966.

Hyde, Montgomery. *Mexican Empire: The History of Maximilian and Carlota of Mexico.* London: Macmillan & Company, Ltd., 1946.

Islas García, Luis. *Apuntes para el estudio del caciquismo en México.* México: Editorial Jus, 1962.

Johnson, Ludwell H. *Red River Campaign: Politics and Cotton in the Civil War.* Baltimore: Johns Hopkins Press, 1958.

Johnson, Richard A. *The Mexican Revolution of Ayutla, 1854-1855: An Analysis of the Evolution and Destruction of Santa Anna's Last Dictatorship.* Rock Island, Ill.: Augustana College Library, 1939.

Lea, Tom. *The King Ranch.* Boston: Little, Brown & Company, 1957. 2 vols.

Lister, Florence C., and Lister, Robert H. *Chihuahua: Storehouse of Storms.* Albuquerque: University of New Mexico Press, 1966.

McCampbell, Coleman. *Saga of a Frontier Seaport.* Dallas: South-West Press, 1934.

Martin, Percy F. *Maximilian in Mexico: The Story of the French Intervention (1861-1867).* London: Constable & Company, Ltd., 1914.

Merk, Frederick. *Manifest Destiny and Mission in American History.* New York: Alfred A. Knopf, 1963.

Morales Gómez, Antonio. *Cronología de Nuevo León, 1527-1955.* México: Editorial Benito Juárez, 1955.

Nance, Joseph Milton. *After San Jacinto: The Texas-Mexican Frontier, 1836-1841.* Austin: University of Texas Press, 1963.

————. *Attack and Counterattack: The Texas-Mexican Frontier, 1842.* Austin: University of Texas Press, 1964.

Naranjo, Leopoldo (ed.). *Lampazos, sus hombres, su tiempo, sus obras.* Monterrey: Talleres J. Cantú Leal, 1934.

Nichols, James L. *The Confederate Quartermaster in the Trans-Mississippi.* Austin: University of Texas Press, 1964.

Nunn, W. C. *Escape From Reconstruction.* Fort Worth: Texas Christian University Press, 1956.

Owsley, Frank Lawrence. *King Cotton Diplomacy: Foreign Relations of the Confederate States of America.* 2nd ed. rev. Chicago: University of Chicago Press, 1959.

Parks, Joseph Howard. *General Edmund Kirby Smith, C. S. A.* Baton Rouge: Louisiana State University Press, 1954.

Remos y Rubio, Juan J. *Resumen de historia de la literatura cubana.* La Habana: Tipos-Molina y Cia., 1945.

Rippy, J. Fred. *The United States and Mexico.* New York: Alfred A. Knopf, 1926.

Riva Palacio, Vicente. *México a través de los siglos.* Barcelona: Editorial de España y Comp., 1888-1889. 5 vols.

Roeder, Ralph. *Juárez and His Mexico.* New York: The Viking Press, 1947. 2 vols.

Roel, Santiago. *Nuevo León: apuntes históricos.* 11th ed. Monterrey: Talleres Linotipográficos del Estado, 1963.

Saldaña, José P. *Historia y tradiciones de Monterrey.* Monterrey: Impresora Monterrey, S.A., 1943.

Saldívar, Gabriel. *Historia Compendiada de Tamaulipas.* México: Editorial Beatriz de Silva, 1945.

Scholes, Walter V. *Mexican Politics During the Juárez Regime, 1855-1872.* Columbia: University of Missouri Studies, 1957.

Sierra, Justo. *Juárez, su obra y su tiempo*. México: Universidad Nacional Autónoma de México, 1956.

Smart, Charles Allen. *Viva Juárez! The Founder of Modern Mexico*. Philadelphia: J. B. Lippincott Company, 1963.

Texas Almanac for 1868. Galveston: W. Richardson & Company, 1868.

Thompson, Samuel Bernard. *Confederate Purchasing Operations Abroad*. Chapel Hill: University of North Carolina Press, 1935.

Webb, Walter P. *The Texas Rangers: A Century of Frontier Defense*. Boston: Houghton-Mifflin Company, 1935.

Webb, Walter P., and Carroll, H. Bailey (eds.). *The Handbook of Texas*. Austin: Texas State Historical Association, 1952. 2 vols.

Velázquez, Primo Feliciano. *Historia de San Luis Potosí*. México: Sociedad Mexicana de Geografía y Estadística, 1947. 4 vols.

Vernon, Raymond. *The Dilemma of Mexico's Development: The Roles of the Private and Public Sectors*. Cambridge: Harvard University Press, 1965.

Vizcaya Canales, Isidro. *Los orígenes de la industrialización de Monterrey (1867-1920)*. Monterrey: Instituto Tecnológico y de Estudios Superiores de Monterrey, 1969.

Zamaçois, Niceto de. *Historia de Méjico*. Méjico: J. F. Parres y Comp., 1877-1882. 18 vols.

Zayas Enríquez, Rafael de. *Benito Juárez, su vida—su obra*. México: Tipografía de la Viuda de Francisco Díaz de León, 1906.

Zorrilla, Luis G. *Historia de las relaciones entre México y los Estados Unidos de América, 1800-1958*. México: Editorial Porrúa, S.A., 1965. 2 vols.

ARTICLES

Acuña, Rudolph F. "Ignacio Pesqueira: Sonoran Caudillo," *Arizona and the West*, XII (Summer, 1970), 139-172.

Bernath, Stuart L. "Squall Across the Atlantic: The Peterhoff Episode," *Journal of Southern History*, XXXIV (August, 1968), 382-383.

Berrueto Ramón, Federico. "Santiago Vidaurri y el estado de Nuevo León y Coahuila," *Humánitas*, VI (1965), 407-421.

Binkley, William C. "New Mexico and the Texan Santa Fé Expedition," *Southwestern Historical Quarterly*, XXVII (October, 1923), 85-107.

Blumenthal, Henry. "Confederate Diplomacy: Popular Notions and International Realities," *Journal of Southern History*, XXXII (May, 1966), 151-171.

Broussard, Ray F. "Vidaurri, Juárez and Comonfort's Return from Exile," *Hispanic American Historical Review*, XLIX (May, 1969), 268-280.

Cohen, Barry M. "The Texas-Mexico Border, 1858-1867," *Texana*, VI (Summer, 1968), 153-165.

Davenport, Harbert. "General José María Jesús Carabajal," *Southwestern Historical Quarterly*, LV (April, 1952), 475-483.

————. "Notes on Early Steamboating on the Rio Grande," *Southwestern Historical Quarterly*, XLIX (October, 1945), 286-289.

Delaney, Robert W. "Matamoros, Port for Texas During the Civil War," *Southwestern Historical Quarterly*, LVIII (April, 1955), 473-487.

Diamond, William. "Imports of the Confederate Government from Europe and Mexico," *Journal of Southern History*, VI (November, 1940), 470-503.

Hall, Martin Hardwick. "Colonel James Reily's Diplomatic Missions to Chihuahua and Sonora," *New Mexico Historical Review*, XXXI (July, 1956), 232-242.

Hanna, Kathryn Abbey. "The Roles of the South in the French Intervention in Mexico," *Journal of Southern History*, XX (February, 1954), 3-21.

Hernández Rodríguez, Rosaura. "Comonfort y la intervención francesa," *Historia Mexicana*, XIII (julio-septiembre, 1963), 59-75.

Lancaster-Jones, Ricardo. "Don Francisco de Paula Verea, Obispo de Linares y de Puebla," *Humánitas*, VII (1966), 395-416.

Larios, Avila. "Brownsville-Matamoros: Confederate Lifeline," *Mid-America*, XL (April, 1958), 67-89.

Mauro, Frédéric. "L'economie du nord-est et la résistance à l'empire," in Arturo Arnaiz y Freg and Claude Bataillon (eds.). *La intervención francesa y el imperio de Maximiliano*. México: Asociación Mexicana de Historiadores Instituto Francés de América Latina, 1965. 61-69.

McCornack, Richard Blaine. "Los Estados Confederados y México," *Historia Mexicana*, IV (julio, 1954-junio, 1955), 337-352.

————. "Juárez y la armada Norteamericana," *Historia Mexicana*, VI (julio, 1956-junio, 1957), 493-509.

Moseley, Edward H. "Indians From the Eastern United States and the Defense of Northeastern Mexico: 1855-1864," *Southwestern Social Science Quarterly*, LXVI (December, 1965), 273-280.

————. "Santiago Vidaurri, Champion of States' Rights: 1855-1857," *West Georgia College Studies in the Social Sciences*, VI (June, 1967), 69-80.

————. "Santiago Vidaurri: heroe de la reforma," *Humánitas*, XI (1970), 685-695.

Neira Barragán, Manuel. "El folklore en el noreste de México durante la intervención francesa," in Ángel Basols Batalla et al. *Temas y figuras de la intervención*. México: Sociedad Mexicana de Geografía y Estadística, 1963. 31-85.

Porter, Kenneth W. "The Seminole in Mexico, 1850-1861," *Hispanic American Historical Review*, XXXI (February, 1951), 1-36.

————. "Wild Cat's Death and Burial," *Chronicles of Oklahoma*, XXI (March, 1943), 41-43.

Ramsdell, Charles W. "The Texas State Military Board, 1862-1865," *Southwestern Historical Quarterly*, XXVII (April, 1924), 253-275.

Shearer, Ernest C. "The Callahan Expedition, 1855," *Southwestern Historical Quarterly*, LIV (April, 1951), 430-451.

————. "The Carvajal Disturbances," *Southwestern Historical Quarterly*, LV (October, 1951), 201-230.

Smith, Mitchell. "The 'Neutral' Matamoros Trade, 1861-1865," *Southwest Review*, XXXVII (Autumn, 1952), 319-324.

Tyler, Ronnie C. "Cotton on the Border, 1861-1865," *Southwestern Historical Quarterly*, LXXIII (April, 1970), 456-477.

————. "Santiago Vidaurri and the Confederacy," *The Americas*, XXVI (July, 1969), 66-76.

————. "The Callahan Expedition of 1855: Indians or Negroes?" *Southwestern Historical Quarterly*, LXX (April, 1967), 574-585.

Weinert, Richard P. "Confederate Border Troubles with Mexico," *Civil War Times Illustrated*, III (October, 1964), 36-43.

Windham, William T. "The Problem of Supply in the Trans-Mississippi Confederacy," *Journal of Southern History*, XXII (May, 1961), 149-168.

DISSERTATIONS AND THESES

Broussard, Ray F. "Ignacio Comonfort: His Contributions to the Mexican Reform, 1855-1857." Ph.D. dissertation, University of Texas, Austin, 1959.

Graf, LeRoy P. "Economic History of the Lower Rio Grande Valley, 1820-1875." Ph.D. dissertation, Harvard University, 1942. 2 vols.

Greer, Viola Ann. "Santiago Vidaurri, Cacique of Northern Mexico: His Relationship to Benito Juárez." M.A. thesis, University of Texas, Austin, 1949.

BIBLIOGRAPHY

Irby, James A. "Line of the Rio Grande: War and Trade on the Confederate Frontier, 1861-1865." Ph.D. dissertation, University of Georgia, 1969.

Moseley, Edward H. "The Public Career of Santiago Vidaurri, 1855-1858." Ph.D. dissertation, University of Alabama, 1963.

as commander of French at Veracruz, 131

Louisiana: as boundary of Spanish territory, 14

Love Bird, H.M.S.: captured by Union, 150

Lubbock, Francis R.: as governor of Texas, 57; Vidaurri writes to, 67; Quintero writes to, 70–71, 83, 101

Luckett, Philip N.: as Confederate commander at Brownsville, 66

Madero, Evaristo: as partner of Milmo, 116; trade contract of, 124; Confederates seize shipment of, 126

Magruder, John Bankhead: problem referred to, 90; detains cotton, 119; hosts Vidaurri in Houston, 142

Manifest Destiny: of North, 41; and northern Mexico, 53

manufacturing: supported by Vidaurri, 29; data on, wanted by South, 56

María de Llano, Manuel: as governor of Nuevo León, 16

María Iglesias, José: as Juárez's minister of hacienda, 137

María Lacunza, José: to be member of prospective regency, 154; replaces Vidaurri, 155

María Ortega, José: as military chieftain, 16

María Patoni, José: as governor of Durango, deposes Terrazas, 146

Marks & Company. *See* K. Marks & Company

Marmaduke, John S.: as Confederate general, 149

Márquez, Leonardo: leads conservative guerrillas, 130; joins French, 131; sent to Mexico City, 154; defeated at Puebla, 155; escapes to Mexico City, 155

Martínez, Domingo: elected governor of Nuevo León, 37, 37 n

Martínez, Pedro: follows Santos Degollado, 36

Masons: Ignacio Comonfort a member of, 59; write letter on behalf of Comonfort, 60 n

Massachusetts: as location of Harvard College, 46 n

Matamoros, Tamaulipas: filibusters at, 21; propaganda from, 25; importing house at, 29 n, 98; dispatches confiscated at, 44; Quintero in, 47, 94, 149; business firms in, 54, 127; goods deposited at, 55, 114; controlled by Vidaurri, 56; decline of trade in, 62, 64, 101, 104; Carvajal near, 63; Carvajal attacks, 63 n; Julián Quiroga sent to, 66; Union consul in, 70; duty on cotton at, 74, 111; *comandante* at, 75; Quintero returns from, 78; Union refugees in, 83, 86; citizens of, support Juárez, 87; governor threatens to arrest Southerners in, 90; Unionist threat at, 91; British consul in, 99; during Mexican War, 102; trade in, 102, 105; Tampico as alternate port of entry to, 103; and cotton, 106–107, 110, 113, 122; Confederates in, 108, 143; speculation in, 112; French to capture, 115; L. Werlman businessman at, 116; government inspector at, 117; Albino López merchant at, 118; Confederate trade routes severed to, 119; Confederate goods moved to, 120; pro-Juárez force controls, 121; Confederate treasury agent in, 123; French expected in, 126, 133–135; revenue from, 136–137, 140; French capture, 147; as good trade location, 148; goods shipped through, 150

131; and Mexican intervention, 132; and trade with South, 148, 151

Naranjo, Francisco: as liberal in Nuevo León politics, 17; and Vidaurri, 18, 36

National Guard (Nuevo León): Vidaurri maintains, 37

nationalism: Mexican, 41

natural resources: needed by South, 49; in Mexico, 50, 52, 56; price of, 54; along proposed railroad route, 55

Negrete, Miguel: arrests Milmo, 142; Juárez supports, 142–143

Negroes. See fugitive slaves

New Mexico: Unionists in, 97; boundary between Texas and, 109

New Orleans, Louisiana: Quintero consul and newspaper editor in, 46 n; L. B. Cain of, 53, 58; Mexican consul in, 60; Masons in, 60 n; Oliver and Brothers contact in, 99; Sandborn and Doen in, 108; as delivery point for cotton, 114

newspapers: Vidaurri confers with editors of, 154

New York City, New York: as important port in U.S., 102; arms ordered from, 115

New York *Herald*: correspondent in Matamoros, 98, 102, 107, 116

norteños: as Vidaurri's army, 32; support Vidaurri, 40–41; in the *Ciudadela*, 139; surrender to Juárez, 142. *See also* northerners (Mexican)

North, Thomas: as Union refugee in Matamoros, 83

northerners (Mexican): and Vidaurri, 16, 19; Vidaurri pleads for support of, 35; Vidaurri as one of, 38. *See also norteños*

northern frontier: *See* northern Mexico

northern Mexico: and Texas, 14; republic in, 22; Republic of Sierra

Madre in, 25, 52; Vidaurri controls, 31, 128; Vidaurri and, 34, 64, 153; possible Union invasion through, 44; 49, 57; as vital area for trade, 45; South's only trade outlet, 51; Confederate annexation of, 53, 56–57; Confederacy and, 62; Carvajal invades, 63 n; trade with, 71; Arthur J. L. Fremantle in, 98; economy of, transformed, 152

novitiates: 35

Nuevo León, Mexico: governor of, 13, 26; Vidaurri controls, 15, 25, 39; liberals in, aid Vidaurri, 18; people of, 19–20; 33, 141, 143; and Coahuila united, 21; reaction to seizure of, 22; president of supreme court of, 32; Vidaurri returns to, 37; Vidaurri as head of, 39; Vidaurri reportedly expelled from 58; Comonfort in, 59; village in, raided, 74; conservative support in, 135; separated from Coahuila, 140; French occupy, 147

Nuevo León militia: Comonfort commands, 59. *See also* army (Nuevo León)

Nuevo León y Coahuila, Mexico: Santiago Vidaurri governor of, 13; Juárez needs customs revenues of, 13; formation of, 27; revised constitution of, 28; administration of, 29; Vidaurri rules, 31, 40; Vidaurri and people of, 33, 141; extradition treaty of, proposed with Texas, 34; Vidaurri's hopes for, 36; Aramberri acting governor of, 36; permission to invade through, discussed, 49; arms unavailable in, 53; annexation of, by South, 58, 78; and Tamaulipas, 61; Southern trade with, 66; annexation by Confederacy proposed, 78; adjacent to Texas, 82; and cotton trade, 99, 107, 110; Vi-

INDEX

Revolution of Ayutla. *See* Ayutla, Revolution of

Reynosa, Tamaulipas: attacked by Carvajal, 70–71; declared free port of entry, 110

Richmond, Virginia: Quintero returns to, 47, 52; Confederate capital, 48, 149; Quintero leaves, 58; Quintero delivers Vidaurri's messages to, 67; José Oliver in, 99–100

Río del Nombre de Dios: in Durango, 55

Rio Grande: as U.S.–Mexican border, 14, 49, 62, 74, 86, 91, 97, 114, 149; trouble along, 20–21; defense of, 48; Roma, Texas, on, 54; ferries on, blocked, 63; trade on, 99, 106; freight costs to, 104; description of, 107; as trade outlet, 128, 150; Vidaurri crosses, 142

Rio Grande City, Texas: and trade, 104–105, 114

Rio Grande Valley: Union to occupy, 95; Confederate agent in, 122

Río Pánuco: harbor at, 103

Ripley, Mrs. Eliza Moore McHatton: quoted, 105

Roel, Santiago: as Vidaurri's biographer, 16

Rogers, L. M.: quoted, 105

rojos: Carvajal commands, 61; in conflict with *amarillos*, 63; cross into Texas, 66; artillery taken, 67; aided by Texans, 70; disbanded, 75

Roma, Texas: and trade goods, 54, 57, 99, 127; on the Rio Grande, 104

Rosas Landa, Vicente: meets with Vidaurri, 26–27

Ruiz, Manuel: governor of Tamaulipas, 120; defeated by Cortina, 121

runaway slaves. *See* fugitive slaves

Runnels, Hardin R.: as governor of

Texas, 34; and extradition treaty with northern Mexico, 34, 50

Russell, Charles: as quartermaster at Brownsville, 114; negotiates with merchants, 114; works with Patricio Milmo, 122–123; relieved of position, 127

Russell, John: as British foreign minister, 130

rustlers: problem to Vidaurri, 28

Sabinas road: Quiroga camped on, 146

Saligny, Dubois de: as French minister in Mexico, 131

Saltillo, Coahuila: Juárez in, 14, 121, 126, 135–136, 138, 140–141; Francisco Güitián approaches, 21; Zuazua killed near, 37; Ibernia factory at, 110; Juárez goes to, 139

saltpeter: South needs, 49–50, 57; deposits of, near Piedras Negras, 54; José Oliver offers, 99; in Zacatecas, 100; price rises on, 101; Governor Morehead discusses trade of, 144

San Antonio, Texas: Spanish-language newspaper in, 46; John S. Ford in, 67; Henry F. McCulloch in, 83; forts near, 97; and trade, 100, 126–127, 151; prospective railroad from, 104; on route to Mexico, 105; newspaper in, quoted, 109; Simeon Hart in, 114, 122; treasury notes en route to, 123; A. Urbahan in, 125

San Camilo Street, Mexico City: Vidaurri captured on, 155

Sandborn and Doen: New Orleans firm, 108

San Luis Potosí, Mexico: offered *Plan de Monterrey*, 21; and *Plan de Ayutla*, 22; captured, 23 n, 27; captured by Vidaurri, 32; atrocities in, 33; Vidaurri leaves, 33; Vidaurri respected in, 61; price of cotton in, 111; Juárez in, 132, 152; and pro-

191

trade, 110; competition among, 116; near border entry points, 117
stage lines: to Bagdad from Matamoros, 106
state debt: liquidated by Vidaurri, 29
State Department. *See* Confederate State Department
state militia. *See* Nuevo León militia
State Military Board. *See* Texas Military Board
states' rights: Vidaurri advocates, 13; Confederacy and, 58
Stillman, Charles: trades with Mexicans, 108; John B. Magruder favors, 119; grows wealthy from trade, 151
suffrage: in Nuevo León, 29
Sumpter, Jesse: quoted, 113, 121

Tabor, John: as Brownsville commissioner, 75
Tamaulipas, Mexico: Vidaurri has power in, 15, 56, 61, 108; and *Plan de Monterrey,* 21; officials expelled from, in San Luis Potosí, 22; opposition in, to Vidaurri, 25; Vidaurri returns from, 26; proposed union between Nuevo León and, 27; material from Europe shipped to, 54; Quintero learns of situation in, 62; expedition organizing for, 63; Vidaurri appointed commander of, 64; Serna and, 66, 120; Vidaurri afraid of losing power in, 67; Carvajal suspected of raiding into, 74; governors of, 79; reaction in, to violation of neutrality, 87; conflict in, 94; fugitive slaves to be extradited from, 95; and cotton trade, 99. 107, 117; trade hampered in, 101–102; August Santleben in, 106; *comandante* of, 110, 134; Albino López governor of, 111; Cortina in, 121; in league with other states, 133; officials of, agree, 143; Vidaurri's supporters control, 152

Tampico, Tamaulipas: Milmo in, 29 n; army to occupy, 64; troops in, 70, 94; Confederate trade through, 102; rarely used for trade, 103; closed by French, 112; soon to be under French control, 134
taxes: require Vidaurri's attention, 20; people of Nuevo León unhappy with, 33
Tehuántepec, Mexico: Isthmus of, 132
Terrazas, Luis: and Vidaurri, 49 n; contacted by Union, 78; contacted by Confederacy, 78–79; loyalty of, questionable, 137; in dispute with Juárez, 146
Texan Santa Fé Expedition: captured in New Mexico, 17
Texas: and northern Mexico, 14, 50; Vidaurri in, 17, 36; raids into, 28, 66–67, 87; William R. Henry of, 32; extradition treaty offered to, 34; and trade with Mexico, 39, 63 n, 97; Quintero in Confederate army in, 46; and Union refugees, 47, 83, 86, 91; invasion threat to, 48–49; Quintero going to, 51; governor of, 51, 57, 143; Vidaurri hopes for help from, 53; Vidaurri's exile in, 58; merchants expelled to, 62; Carvajal retreats to, 66; Carvajal organizes troops in, 70; Vidaurri and raiders into, 71, 74; effect of Quintero's resignation threats in, 74; raids by refugees from, 75; Union consul quoted, 82, 98; Nathaniel Banks prepares to invade, 95; possibility of Mexico being cut off from, 97; and cotton trade, 99, 104, 111; blockade of ports in, 101; John Warren Hunter in, quoted, 105; poor trade system in, 109; and Compromise of 1850, 107; flour shipped to, 116; wagon train enters, 118; Hart of, 125; Confederates stop trade from, 125; de-

mand for material from, 148; trade of during French occupation, 148, 151; U.S. Cabinet advocates conquest of, 150

Texas Almanac: Quintero works on, 149; articles by Quintero in, 149 n

Texas Christian University Library: microfilm from, used, 22 n

Texas Military Board: established, 109; controls bonds, 109; controls cotton marketing in state, 109; agents of, in Mexico, 116–117

Texas Rangers: invade Mexico, 24; expel Cortina, 48; with Carvajal and Ford, 63 n

Texas State Gazette (newspaper): published in Austin, 47 n

textile factory. *See* Ibernia and La Fama

Thayer, Clarence C.: as Confederate treasury agent, 123; informs Quintero of seizure of treasury notes, 124

theater: encouraged by Vidaurri, 29

Thompson, R. P.: American Bible Society representative in Mexico, 128

Three Years' War. *See* War of the Reform

Toombs, Robert: as Confederate Secretary of State, 46

Traconis, Juan B.: as governor of Tamaulipas, 111; raises duty, 118

trade: on Santa Fé Trail, 17; decline in, 26, 64, 103; and Vidaurri, 29, 29, 34–35, 74, 78, 97–98, 153; C. B. H. Blood and, 79; Vidaurri on, to Juárez, 82; López and, 90, 118; cotton in, 98–99, 101–102; fear of speculators in, 100; companies in, 100, 127; obstacles to Mexican, 101; Chase on, 103; between Confederacy and Mexico, 106, 108, 119, 149–150; mismanagement of, 116; disruption of, 121–122, 146; Kimmey on, 127; Juárez and, 140, 144;

during French occupation, 148–149, 151; prosperity as result of, 151–152

trade goods: en route to Gulf of Mexico, 15, 150; tariff levied on, 51; exchanged between Texas and Mexico, 97; fees collected from, 98; Confederate government needs, 111; specie demanded for, 113; from Mexico, 115–116, 141; demanded in Texas, 148; purchased by Confederate agent, 151

trade routes: Union severance of, 95, 119; through Texas, 104–105, 121

Trans-Mississippi Department. *See* Confederate Trans-Mississippi Department

transportation: as problem for South, 54–55, 101, 104, 106

Treviño & Company: or Trevins & Company, 54 n; and Mifflin Kenedy, 70

Treviño, Manuel: as Mexican consul in Brownsville, 71; recalled, 71 n

Treviño Garza, José María: followed Santos Degollado, 36

Trevins & Company: of Brownsville and Matamoros, 54; correct name of, 54 n

Tucson, Arizona: Union troops in, 97

Tucumcari, New Mexico: Texan Santa Fé Expedition arrested near, 17

Tyler, Texas: newspaper in, quoted, 86

Tyler *Reporter* (newspaper): quoted, 86

United States (Union): Civil War, 15; and Mexican War, 17; admired by Vidaurri, 19, 39; filibusters from, 23; and northern Mexico, 28, 52; extradition treaty with Mexico, 34, 94; blockade of South, 54, 103, 107; prospective war with European country, 43, 58, 150; European country wants counter-balance against, 43 n; and march through Mexico, 49, 57, 78–79; Juárez favors, 71; and Juárez, 82, 140, 153; New York as port for, 102; and Compromise of 1850, 109; invades Brownsville, 122; and Confederacy, 128; Mexican Empire and, 135; Santos Doblado in, 145; and England and France, 152

United States (Union) Army: patrols border, 25; and possible march through Mexico, 44, 49, 51, 57, 78, 86; threat of invasion by, 95; captures Brownsville, 120, 123; threatens Laredo, 141; presses Confederate army, 149

United States Cabinet: advises conquering Texas, 150

United States Constitution: forbids treaties between states, 34

United States (Union) Navy: blockade of the South, 15, 99, 101, 103, 108

University of Texas Newspaper Collection: *Texas State Gazete* in, 47 n

Uraga, José López: betrays Juárez, 145

Urbahan, A.: as merchant in San Antonio, 122; as Milmo's agent, 125

Valle, Leandro: killed by Márquez, 130

Varieties Theater, Matamoros: site of Protestant worship services, 83

Vela, Isidro: murdered, 91

Veracruz, Mexico: U.S. consul in, 44; Spanish troops land in, 131

Victoria, Nuevo León: Ignacio Zaragoza in, 19; route to, 109

Vidaurri, Indalecio: threatens Juárez, 14, 139

Vidaurri, Santiago: and Juárez, 13–14, 31–32, 34, 41, 46, 48, 51–52, 58–59,

64, 79–80, 82, 94, 119, 128–129, 134–142, 145–146, 151, 153; governmental philosophy of, 13, 39; as power in northern Mexico, 13, 15, 32, 61, 64, 128; and French, 13–14, 39, 128–129, 132–137, 140–141, 148, 153; birthplace of, 15–16, 18; early career of, 16–17; in Texas, 17, 36, 47, 58, 142, 147; as liberal, 17; seizes Nuevo León, 17–19; liberals support, 18, 23; as administrator, 19–20, 28–30, 32, 41, 128; and the Church, 20, 30, 31–32, 35; spreads influence, 20–22, 25; and Republic of Sierra Madre, 22, 25, 32, 52; repels Texan invasion, 24; and Álvarez, 24, 26, 28; and annexation of Coahuila, 24–27; invades Tamaulipas, 25; strengthens control over northern states, 25, 31; influence of, in national politics, 27; invades San Luis Potosí, 27, 32; and War of Reform, 30, 34, 38, 138; and reform laws, 30–31, 35; declares Nuevo León y Coahuila independent, 31; conservative opposition to, 32; defeated at Ahualulco, 33; and trade, 34; reinforces position, 34; and the South, 34, 43, 45–61, 64, 66–67, 70–71, 74–75, 78, 82, 87, 97, 114, 119, 124, 126–127, 151–153; and annexation of northern Mexico, 34, 51–53, 57, 78; splits with liberals, 35–38, 135; and Quintero, 36, 45–60, 66–67, 70–71, 74–75, 78, 82–83, 87, 90, 94, 97, 110, 114, 117–118, 124, 126, 153; reelected governor, 37–38; regionalism of, 40; and Terrazas, 49 n; offers supplies to South, 54, 67, 71; desires better transportation, 56; demands loan from merchants, 64, 147; and dispute in Tamaulipas, 64, 66–67, 94, 134; and filibuster problem, 70–71, 74, 82; changes tariff on cotton,